Collaborative Library Research Projects

Collaborative Library Research Projects

Inquiry that Stimulates the Senses

John D. Volkman

A Member of the Greenwood Publishing Group

Westport, Connecticut • London

Library of Congress Cataloging-in-Publication Data

Volkman, John D.
    Collaborative library research projects : inquiry that stimulates
the senses / John D. Volkman.
        p. cm.
    ISBN 978-1-59158-623-4 (alk. paper)
    1. Library orientation for high school students—United States.
2. Library orientation for junior high school students—United States.
3. Research—Methodology—Study and teaching (Secondary) 4. Active
learning—United States—Case studies.   5. School librarian participation
in curriculum planning—United States. I. Title.
    Z711.25.H54V65 2008
    025.5674—dc22   2008000640

British Library Cataloguing in Publication Data is available.

Library of Congress Catalog Card Number: 2008000640
ISBN: 978–1–59158–623–4

First published in 2008

Libraries Unlimited, 88 Post Road West, Westport, CT 06881
A Member of the Greenwood Publishing Group, Inc.
www.lu.com

Printed in the United States of America

The paper used in this book complies with the
Permanent Paper Standard issued by the National
Information Standards Organization (Z39.48–1984).

10 9 8 7 6 5 4 3 2 1

The assignment sheets in the book may be adapted to fit individual libraries and classes. For example, bibliographies with call numbers for specific libraries can be added or lessons may be used as prototypes for similar lessons. To facilitate this process, a CD of the assignment pages in Word format may be obtained by contacting the author:

John Volkman
8380 N. Raisina Avenue
Fresno, CA 93720
559-435-6967 / jvolkman23@comcast.net

To my dad who was the inspiration for my becoming a school librarian. As a World War II veteran of the Battle of the Bulge, he epitomized the "Greatest Generation" in his work ethic, Christian values, and patriotism. He is the one who taught me to be a writer by working with me to write, proofread, and rewrite everything I wrote in school. Thus, he instilled in me the need for perspiration to go with the inspiration

Contents

Acknowledgments

In writing a book about collaborative teaching, it is mandatory to give full credit to the teachers with whom I have worked over the years. The Holocaust unit was developed with Wes Lusher, an English teacher at Hoover High School in Fresno, California. The other units were all done in collaboration with teachers at Reedley High School. As a result of utilizing the Holocaust unit, English teachers Janet Adams and Betsy Harcastle suggested and helped create the units for *To Kill a Mockingbird* and *Animal Farm*, respectively.

English teacher Gitte Trejo was the inspiration for the Edgar Allan Poe unit, the Evil People essay, the Hispanic Biography brochure, and the Odyssey newspaper. The poster project on the *Children of the River* was done with English teacher Ann Brandon. Although not directly involved in any of these units, English Department chair Susan Lusk has been a coordinating force behind her department working closely together with me.

The World War II unit was done at the suggestion of now retired U.S. history teacher Danny Howerton. His active participation in creating the unit, along with the diligent work of his fellow U.S. history teacher, Tony Fernandez, were instrumental in our creation of this award-winning unit.

A number of teachers of freshman science over a period of years helped put together the Constellations and Rocks and Minerals poster projects. These teachers included Lisa Marchese, Mike Evans, and Tony Rotella.

The culminating unit on the Shoebox Float was largely created by World Cultures teacher Roger Hoeflinger. Following his basic lesson plans, we worked together to develop the library research of the unit.

And the inspirational light behind all my library work has been my mother, Beth Volkman, herself a retired high school librarian and voice of support in all my endeavors.

CHAPTER 1

Collaborating with Teachers to Promote Student Research

Students retain more of what they have learned when they have actively engaged in the learning process. To engage students in active learning, it is useful to have them do library units involving "stations." These stations are set up so that students will view, listen, read, interact, and discuss the material. In setting up these stations, librarians and teachers collaborate in deciding which methods will work best for any particular unit.

The first step in collaboration between the teacher and the school librarian is for the teacher to let the librarian know what general topic is to be covered. With the general topic in mind, they can then choose which stations would work for that topic. The librarian presents the teacher with the list of possible of types of stations, including the following:

- Poetry
- Primary sources with drawing
- Audio: music
- Hyperstudio/PowerPoint
- Art/posters

- Video
- Quotations with drawing
- Audio: poetry, reading
- Internet
- Research

With this list in mind, the librarian and the teacher will consider what is available in the library collection, online, and in the teacher's materials as they choose the best stations for that unit. The librarian's knowledge of the library collection and experience from previous units are what makes them an invaluable partner in the collaborative teaching process and the key to developing stimulating units.

If one of the stations is to be a research station, the librarian can develop a list of topics and have the teacher add to and subtract from it. For an Internet station, the librarian can find, evaluate, and select a number of useful websites. For audio stations, the librarian can record the tapes or burn the discs needed for the music, poetry, or oral history involved. The librarian can also play a key role in finding primary sources or locating videos or quotations to use at the appropriate stations. The typical classroom teacher does not have the time or the knowledge of library resources to carry out these roles. The librarian can smoothly carry out these roles as part of being an "information specialist."

Once the stations have been developed, the librarian and teacher can weigh the relative effort and time needed for each station and assign the point values to each station accordingly. The librarian can type up the cover sheet listing the decided-upon point values. With the librarian serving as a point person, the cover sheet can easily be adapted when other teachers want to do the unit but use different point systems. In setting up an attractive cover sheet, it is recommended that pictures of the topic be included on it. These pictures can easily be copied and pasted from the Internet and provide visual appeal and additional points of learning.

In addition to being the driving force behind collaborative lessons, the librarian can be the pivotal person in the school in getting students and teachers to use a uniform method of citing sources and in taking notes. The key concept to sell to the teachers is that by having all the disciplines follow the same formats, the students will get in the habit of citing their sources in the same manner every time they do research. Regardless of the discipline, the points assigned for each research assignment contain a specific list of values for grading each part of the bibliography.

To facilitate this repetition, the use of source pages that have formats for the most commonly used resources—books, websites, and periodical databases—is encouraged. The appendix contains "source pages" for each of these types of resources. Additionally, there are source pages that combine entries for books and Internet sites for assignments that require only a couple of each. If the librarian will supply these in the library for use with all research projects, the teachers and students will get accustomed to always using them. Teachers appreciate having these forms available in the library, which helps in getting the teachers to buy into using them and the uniform bibliography formats suggested.

A uniform way of taking notes from research sources is also strongly encouraged as a method for students to develop a more efficient use of the library and its resources. Chapter 8 of Debbie Stanley's book, *Practical Steps to the Research Process for High School* (1999), explains in depth how to teach the note-taking process. Her "Blank Note Card Template" on page 143 is an excellent one to use. By reducing it in size and putting four "note papers" per 8 1/2" × 11" piece of paper, an easily duplicated "note paper" can be made and supplied to the students for use in all of their research projects. Regardless of whether students use this form for their notes or use cards or lined paper, the key concept to stress is that the source paper is used in conjunction with the note papers by putting on each note the number of the source from the source paper. If the source is a book, the page number used is put after the source number.

Another way to encourage uniformity of citations throughout the disciplines is to supply all of the students with the same bibliography formats page. Appendix 1 shows an example of the various bibliography forms based on the Modern Language Association (MLA) style sheet. Students can be encouraged to keep this format sheet in their binders and to use it whenever they need help in constructing their bibliographies.

CHAPTER 2

World War II Station Unit

The station unit put together by the librarian and a U.S. history teacher on World War II illustrates the collaborative process and the development of the stations. The U.S. history teacher initially indicated to the librarian what general subject needed to be covered. The two of them then brainstormed some possible stations. During the summer a four-CD set of World War II songs was purchased. The help of someone who had lived during the war period was solicited in choosing the most important songs. In the fall, the librarian developed a list of topics for the research station and had the teacher add and subtract from it. The librarian found, evaluated, and then selected a number of useful World War II websites.

The final unit consists of six stations. At station one, students complete maps of World War II locations that reinforce the global nature of the war and help students learn their world geography. At the second station, students do research using both books and the Internet. They use the information they find to create a poster and report, which they present to their class. Students listen to music from the World War II era at station three, where they evaluate the music and lyrics. At station four, students listen to oral history in which a World War II veteran recounts his experiences fighting in the Battle of the Bulge, crossing the Rhine River, and accepting a German unit's surrender. Station five requires the students to use the Internet to find and analyze a cartoon from World War II cartoonist Bill Mauldin. Then they browse the Smithsonian World War II site to find in-depth information on some aspect of the war. At station six, students watch a World War II movie, which gives them a basic framework of the war on which they can build the other information they are learning.

The unit gives the students a chance to learn about the war using a variety of learning modalities. Students like the opportunity to work outside of the classroom and the textbook. Within their groups they need to work both cooperatively and independently so that they must exercise their social and individual motivational skills to do a good job on the assigned work.

U.S. history teacher Tony Fernandez had these reactions to the use of the World War II Station unit:

- The library media unit allows the students to use a variety of sources in the library and get a break from their original classroom routine. The library is set up into six different stations by our librarian, and the teacher is simply a facilitator. The students especially enjoy the opportunity to listen to music and listen to true oral history from the time period. The students are actively engaged in six different stations, all of which cover a variety of learning modalities.
- Cooperative learning is key to this project working, and students learn to cross barriers and work with students they barely know to get tasks accomplished. As the years pass, it seems that students remember the library units above all else. It is a combination of fun and learning that brings out the best in the students. The culmination of the two-week-long project ends with an oral presentation and includes a poster that the students put together with great care. It encourages them to practice their speech skills and gives them an opportunity to "think on their feet" as they are asked questions by the students and instructor.

The first year that the unit was used, each student was required to fill out an evaluation form, from which a number of ideas were garnered to better construct these stations and others. It was interesting to note that in the evaluations, the same stations that some students really liked, others hated, and vice-versa. That underlined how different students learn in different ways, and the importance of providing a variety of ways to learn using the different modalities. Below are a few of the comments from the evaluation sheets:

- "I liked the oral history section because I learned what war was like."
- "I liked the change, and mostly it was an interesting way to learn—hands on."
- "The research was not too easy, but I love learning about people, things, places."
- "I actually enjoyed all the stations. You did an awesome job organizing the stations, Mr. Volkman. Great job."
- "I liked the music station the best. It was interesting to hear music other than I'm used to. It really gave me the feeling of listening to a radio during World War II."
- "I learned the most and liked it because we got to research by our own methods. Creativity came out through poster."

In implementing the World War II unit, libraries will be able to utilize resources that they already have or that are readily available. In doing the book research and filling in the maps, the students were able to select from about 50 books and atlases that were already available on the library shelves. Most libraries would have some books on World War II and could add to them as needed. Students also used computers to find Internet information. They used a CD player and a cassette tape player from the library to listen to songs and oral history using wireless headphones.

Most libraries would also have a suitable World War II video or could readily buy one. Buying CDs of World War II songs would be inexpensive, and finding a local World War II vet for oral history would not involve much expense other than the price of a tape and a recorder. There are many websites that offer World War II oral history that can be used for educational purposes.

When setting up the unit in the library, it is a good idea to display World War II posters and memorabilia in the library. Also, to set the mood for the unit, someone can dress the part of a World War II soldier. It is not hard to find a hat, shirt, gas mask, canteen, and belt at a military surplus store or from fellow teachers or other friends. The students appreciate the extra effort, and it lends a touch of reality and authenticity to the unit.

Before the class comes to the library, the classroom teacher needs to do two things. First, divide the students into six groups, numbered one through six. The students will begin at the station that matches their number and then rotate in order through the stations. Second, the teacher should assign or have the students choose which of the topics they will be researching.

Librarian John Volkman, and U.S. history teacher Tony Fernandez are shown welcoming the students to the library for the stations' unit on World War II. The Nazi flag in the background is an authentic Nazi flag surrendered to Cpl. Ernest R. Volkman by a German unit near the end of the war. It is signed by the men of Cpl. Volkman's platoon and is displayed to remember these men of "the greatest generation" who fought to keep America and the world free from Nazism.

STATION 1: WORLD WAR II RESEARCH

Teacher Instructions

MATERIALS NEEDED

1. Books with information on the World War II topics. Some suggestions:

    Feldman, George. *World War II: Almanac.* Detroit: UXL, 2000. 416p. $110.00. 0–7876–3832–3.

    Hatt, Christine. *World War II, 1939–1945.* New York: Franklin Watts, 2001. 62p. op. 0–531–14612-X.

    History of World War II. New York: Marshall Cavendish, 2005. 3 vols. 960p. $399.93. 0–7614–7482-X.

    The New Grolier Encyclopedia of World War II. New York: Grolier Educational Corporation, 1995. 8 vols. op. 0–7172–7508–6.

    Schneider, Carl J., and Dorothy Schneider. *World War II.* New York: Facts on File, 2003. 472p. (Eyewitness History Series). $75.00. 0–8160–4484–8.

    Tucker, Spencer, ed. *World War II: a Student Encyclopedia.* Santa Barbara, Calif.: ABC-CLIO, 2005. 5 vols. $485. 1–85109–857–7.

    In addition to reference and regular books specifically on World War II, books on U.S. history that cover that time period and books that include information on the persons and events associated with World War II should also be made available.

2. Note papers.

3. Source pages with two books and two Internet sites, see Appendix 4.

STATION CONSTRUCTION

1. Put the books that have been pulled from the shelves on a book cart next to where the station is located. (Hint: locating the station near the copier makes copying convenient and quicker.)

2. Have the note papers as well as additional source pages at the station.

Name _____

Teacher _____

Date _____ Period ____ Group_____

World War II Notebook Cover Sheet

Your notebook will include the following, clearly labeled, in the order given.

Your Points	Possible Points		
_____	40	**Station 1:**	**Research Assignment** ◆ **World War II person/event** ◆ **Report, poster, oral report**
_____	10	**Station 2:**	**Music** ◆ **Listen to CD of popular music of the era** ◆ **Complete ratings sheet** ◆ **Write description of favorite songs**
_____	10	**Station 3:**	**Map Activity** ◆ **Complete map research**
_____	10	**Station 4:**	**Oral History** ◆ **Listen to tape of World War II vet's stories** ◆ **Take notes** ◆ **Draw picture of one incident** ◆ **Write short description**
_____	15	**Station 5:**	**Computer-Timeline Assignment** ◆ **Print out and describe cartoon** ◆ **Describe movie, slideshow, and artifact**
_____	15	**Station 6:**	**Video: World War II** ◆ **Fill in worksheet as you watch video**
_____	100	**Total Points**	
_____		**Your Grade**	

STATION 1: WORLD WAR II RESEARCH

ASSIGNMENT

1. Pretend you are a reporter during World War II.
2. Write a 1–2 page article explaining the significance of your topic in relationship to World War II.
3. Include a Bibliography/Works Cited listing your sources in correct format.
4. Present an oral report (2–3 minutes) to the class on your topic.
5. Make a poster that explains important aspects of your topic.

TOPICS

1.	Appeasement	23.	Hitler, Adolf
2.	Atomic bomb	24.	Isolationists
3.	Bataan Death March	25.	Kamikaze
4.	Battle of Britain	26.	MacArthur, Douglas
5.	Battle of the Atlantic	27.	Marshall, George
6.	Berlin, Fall of	28.	Midway
7.	Blitzkrieg	29.	Montgomery, Bernard
8.	Bradley, Omar	30.	Navajo Code Talkers
9.	Bulge, Battle of	31.	Patton, George
10.	Chamberlin, Neville	32.	Pearl Harbor, Attack on
11.	Chiang Kai-shek	33.	Prisoners of War
12.	Churchill, Winston	34.	Rationing
13.	Coral Sea	35.	Resistance Movements
14.	D-Day	36.	Rommel, Erwin
15.	DeGaulle, Charles	37.	Roosevelt, Franklin D.
16.	Eichmann, Adolf	38.	Stalin, Joseph
17.	Fall of the Philippines	39.	Stalingrad, Battle of
18.	France, Fall of	40.	Truman, Harry
19.	German SS	41.	U-Boats
20.	Goebbells, Joseph	42.	Victory Gardens
21.	Goerring, Hermann	43.	WAVES
22.	Hirohito	44.	Women on the Home Front

RESEARCH STEPS

1. Find and use at least one book and one Internet source on your topic. Minimum of:

   • Six notes from a book
   • Six notes from Internet source.

2. Record bibliographic information for each source.
3. Use the library website or search engines for Internet sources.

POSTER REQUIREMENTS

1. Size: 28" × 22"
2. Contents:

    • Photos, drawings, maps, cartoons of pertinent people, events, places
    • Appropriate typed captions in your own words for each picture
    • Short, word-processed information describing topic.

3. Your name in the lower right-hand corner of the front side.
4. On back side write two questions that other students should be able to answer after reading your poster.

GRADING

1.	1–2 page article	10 points	_____
2.	Note cards/bibliography	(10 points)	
	• Sources all in one list alphabetically	1 point	_____
	• Book sources in proper form	3 points	_____
	• Internet sources in proper form	3 points	_____
	• Minimum of 12 note papers	3 points	_____
3.	Poster	10 points	_____
4.	Oral Presentation	10 points	_____
5.	Total	40 points	_____

World War II Poster Example

1. Size: 28" × 22"

NORTH AFRICAN CAMPAIGN

American General
Eisenhower relaxes.

2. Title:
Place a title at
the top using
the name of
your topic in
large letters.

3. Pictures:
Use photos or
drawings of
people,
events, places

4. Captions:
Type
appropriate
captions for
each picture

**5. Written
Information:**
Include important
facts, quotations in
brief, typed form

Written information could go here:
Lieutenant-General Dwight Eisenhower and
Major General Patton were in charge of
Operation Torch.

More written information
could go
here:_____
_____
_____
_____

The defeat at Tunisia cost
Hitler 250,000 men.

"... forever. Amen. Hit the dirt."

Bill Mauldin Cartoon

Juan Trejo Per. 3

**6. More Written
information:**
Include important
facts and quotations
in brief, typed form

**7. Timeline,
map, or chart**

**8. Bill Mauldin
WW II cartoon
with caption**

9. Questions:
On bottom left of
back side write 2
questions that can
be answered by
viewing your
board.

10. Name:
Place your
name in the
lower right-
hand corner.

General Marshall

"...forever, Amen. Hit the dirt." Cartoon:
Copyright 1944 by Bill Mauldin.
Couresy of the Mauldin Estate.

STATION 2: WORLD WAR II SONGS

Teacher Instructions

MATERIALS NEEDED

1.   CDs of World War II songs
2.   Listening stations with headsets and CD player
3.   Computer with CD burner
4.   Websites with World War II song lyrics

STATION CONSTRUCTION

CD collections of songs from the World War II era are readily available in stores and online. Choose songs from them that were the most recognizable or significant songs of that time. If possible, get someone who lived during that time to help choose the songs; they will love doing it. My mother helped me and really enjoyed the trip down memory lane.

From the CDs, choose enough to fill about 25–28 minutes and then burn them to a single CD. To enable the students to primarily listen and enjoy the music, simply have them rate the songs and write brief reactions. A paragraph or two summarizing their reactions to their best-liked or most meaningful songs would be all that is required as the end product.

The lyrics to most of the songs can be found by doing an Internet search for World War II song lyrics or for the specific song itself. Here are two sites that are helpful in finding the lyrics: http://kclibrary.nhmccd.edu/music-2.html and http://www.theromantic.com/patrioticlyrics/main.htm.

Copy and paste these lyrics onto a sheet that the students can use to follow the words of the songs. It is best to laminate multiple copies of the sheet so that each person at the station can follow along.

STATION 2: WORLD WAR II SONGS

RATE A RECORD

On scale of 1 to 5 with 1 being lowest and 5 the highest, rate each song according to how much you liked the tune and the lyrics. Also, give your reaction to each song.

Arms for the Love of America: Barry Wood (no lyrics) (1941) (1:16)

    1 2 3 4 5 Tune   1 2 3 4 5 Lyrics   Reaction:

Army Air Corps (The Air Force Song) (1942) (2:43)

    1 2 3 4 5 Tune   1 2 3 4 5 Lyrics   Reaction:

Boogie Woogie Bugle Boy: Andrews Sisters (1941) (2:44)

    1 2 3 4 5 Tune   1 2 3 4 5 Lyrics   Reaction:

Comin' In on a Wing and a Prayer: The 4 Vagabonds (1943) (2:00)

    1 2 3 4 5 Tune   1 2 3 4 5 Lyrics   Reaction:

G. I. Jive: Johnny Mercer (1943) (1:59)

    1 2 3 4 5 Tune   1 2 3 4 5 Lyrics   Reaction:

Here Comes the Navy: Andrews Sisters (no lyrics) (1942) (1:47)

    1 2 3 4 5 Tune   1 2 3 4 5 Lyrics   Reaction:

Keep 'Em Flying: Gene Krupa (1941) (2:54)

    1 2 3 4 5 Tune   1 2 3 4 5 Lyrics   Reaction:

On the Atchison, Topeka and the Santa Fe: Johnny Mercer (1944) (1:32)

    1 2 3 4 5 Tune   1 2 3 4 5 Lyrics   Reaction:

Praise the Lord and Pass the Ammunition!: Nelson Eddy (1942) (1:42)

      1 2 3 4 5 Tune   1 2 3 4 5 Lyrics   Reaction:

Sentimental Journey: Doris Day (1944) (2:00)

      1 2 3 4 5 Tune   1 2 3 4 5 Lyrics   Reaction:

Tell It to the Marines: Kay Kyser (1941) (2:40)

      1 2 3 4 5 Tune   1 2 3 4 5 Lyrics   Reaction:

U.S. Marine Corps Hymn: Al Goodman's Orchestra (1941) (0:57)

      1 2 3 4 5 Tune   1 2 3 4 5 Lyrics   Reaction:

Vict'ry Polka: Bing Crosby and the Andrews Sisters (1943) (2:02)

      1 2 3 4 5 Tune   1 2 3 4 5 Lyrics   Reaction:

We Must Be Vigilant (No lyrics) (1942) (1:16)

      1 2 3 4 5 Tune   1 2 3 4 5 Lyrics   Reaction:

The White Cliffs of Dover: Kate Smith (1941) (1:34)

      1 2 3 4 5 Tune   1 2 3 4 5 Lyrics   Reaction:

You're in the Army Now: The Jesters (no lyrics) (1941) (1:31)

      1 2 3 4 5 Tune   1 2 3 4 5 Lyrics   Reaction:

On separate paper describe in about a half-page which song or songs you liked best and why they were meaningful to you.

STATION 3: WORLD WAR II MAP

Teacher Instructions

MATERIALS NEEDED

1. Outline map of World War II showing European, Asian, and African theaters
2. Colored pencils or markers
3. Historical atlases such as:

Goldstein, Margaret J. *World War II: Europe.* Minneapolis: Lerner, 2004. 96p. $27.93. 0–8225–0139–2.

Hammond Atlas of United States History. Union, NJ: Hammond, 2001. $16.95. 72p. 0–8437–1449–2.

Hammond Concise Atlas of World History. Maplewood, N.J.: Hammond, 1998. 184p. op. 0–8437–1121–3.

Hammond Historical World Atlas. Union, NJ: Hammond, 2000. 72p. $11.95. 0–8437–1390–9.

Natkiel, Richard. *Atlas of American Wars.* New York: Arch Cape Press, 1986. 160p. op. 0–517–44286–8.

Natkiel, Richard. *Atlas of Battles.* New York: Military Press, 1984. 159p. op. 0–517–44286–8.

4. World War II maps in books or encyclopedias

STATION CONSTRUCTION

Pull atlases from the library shelves and stack them on the table where the students will work on this station.

Put a small box with a variety of colored pencils in it on the table.

STATION 3: WORLD WAR II MAP

1. *Label* the following countries as they appeared in 1942 at the height of Axis power. *Color* them as follows: one color for "Allied countries," one for "Axis countries," and one for "Axis-occupied countries."

Belgium	France
Poland	Soviet Union
China	United Kingdom
Norway	Japan
Germany	Finland
Italy	Libya
Australia	Burma
Egypt	

2. *Label* and/or draw the following bodies of water:

Atlantic Ocean	Pacific Ocean
Rhine River	North Sea
Mediterranean Sea	Baltic Sea
English Channel	Indian Ocean
South China Sea	

3. *Locate* on your map with a *dot* and *label* the following battles and cities:

London	Berlin
Stalingrad	Normandy
Battle of the Bulge	Hiroshima
El Alamein	Guadalcanal
Midway	Manila, Philippines
Iwo Jima	Tokyo
Okinawa	Sicily
Leyte Gulf	Pearl Harbor
Sicily	

Sources

1. *Atlas of Battles,* pp. 57–135
2. *World War II: Europe,* pp. 86–87
3. *Atlas of American Wars,* pp. 72–141
4. *Hammond Historical World Atlas,* pp. H49–H50
5. *Hammond Concise Atlas of World History,* pp. 132–135
6. *Hammond Atlas of United States History,* pp. U46–U49

Cpl. Ernest R. Volkman (age 19) in Germany around the time of the Battle of the Bulge.

STATION 4: WORLD WAR II—ORAL HISTORY

Teacher Instructions

MATERIALS NEEDED

1. CD of World War II oral history
2. Listening stations with headsets and CD player
3. Computer with CD/DVD burner
4. Websites with World War II oral history and/or video history

STATION CONSTRUCTION

Ideally, there may still be a World War II veteran in your community who could be interviewed and his/her story made a part of the project. Another option is to use one of the many websites that offer oral histories from World War II veterans. These oral histories are available in audio, video, and transcript form. Some of the sites that offer these oral histories are listed here:

http://oralhistory.minds.tv/about.asp
http://oralhistory.rutgers.edu/home.html
http://thedropzone.org/oss/default.asp
http://www.au.af.mil/au/awc/awcgate/awc-hist.htm#wwii
http://www.si.umich.edu/CHICO/oralhistory/links.html

My father, Ernest R. Volkman, was a paratrooper in World War II and fought in the Battle of the Bulge. As youngsters growing up, my brother, my cousins, and I often begged to hear his "war stories." At the suggestion of a friend, I recorded those stories on cassette tape in 1989. Because my dad passed away in 2005, I was extremely grateful to have recorded those stories when I did, and to be able to bring them to life again for this World War II station. I have subsequently put them on CD. They can be obtained for a nominal cost by contacting me via my e-mail address: jvolkman23@comcast.net, or by contacting me via the Libraries Unlimited website: http://lu.com.

The students listen to the stories and take notes on the form shown on the next page. To aid the students in taking notes and focusing on each story, it is helpful to supply partial or outline notes on which the students can build. The following is a sample using the Volkman CD; teachers can construct their own using stories found on websites or other sources.

The pictures of Cpl. Ernest R. Volkman can be copied and laminated and posted at the station so that the students can see what he looked like, and that he was a real person, not much older then than they are now.

ORAL HISTORY—CPL. ERNEST R. VOLKMAN (1925–2005)

Listen to the tape. The keywords on the left refer to experiences described in the order they occur. As you listen, jot down some notes to help you remember key events. You will use the notes to write a brief paper.

Keywords	**Your Notes**

Enlistment and Induction

Recruiting station
Training
Paratrooper

Training

River crossing
504 Regiment
Battle of the Bulge

Patrol/Rescue of Sgt. Hamm

Lead scouting party
Sgt. Hamm
Shoots Germans
"Where were you guys?" "Volkman, are you nuts?"
"Any Americans out there?"

River Crossing

Row across Rhine River
"Are we going to run?"
"Rest later!"

Surrender of Germans

Germans surrender
Trepidation (fear)
German lugars and flags

Life/Temptations As a Soldier

Immorality
Drinking beer

DRAW A GRAPHIC AND WRITE A DESCRIPTION

Choose one of the incidents that Corporal Volkman tells about and draw a graphic illustrating what happened. In your graphic use (a) *color,* (b) *symbols,* and (c) *words* to explain what is portrayed. Give your graphic a title.

Write 1/2–1 page description of this incident using your notes. Include what happened and your reaction to what occurred.

STATION 5: WORLD WAR II—CARTOONS/TIMELINE/ARTIFACTS

Teacher Instructions

MATERIALS NEEDED

Computers with Internet access.

STATION CONSTRUCTION

Students will be using a couple of World War II-related websites for this station. It would facilitate student access to these websites if they are posted to the library website. Students will click on the websites and follow the directions on the worksheet.

STATION 5: WORLD WAR II—CARTOONS/TIMELINE/ARTIFACTS

WORLD WAR II CARTOONS

Click on the link: http://ww2.pstripes.osd.mil/02/nov02/mauldin/

Bill Mauldin joined the U.S. army in 1940 and began producing cartoons for the *45th Division News*. He took part in the invasions of Sicily and Italy in 1943. The next year he became a full-time cartoonist for the *Stars and Stripes*. His cartoons often featured two infantrymen named Willie and Joe.

Ernie Pyle, America's most popular journalist in World War II, wrote a favorable review of Mauldin's work and soon his cartoons began appearing in newspapers all over the United States. He later recalled that "I drew pictures for and about the soldiers because I knew what their life was like and understood their gripes. I wanted to make something out of the humorous situations which come up even when you don't think life could be any more miserable."

In 1945, Mauldin's cartoons on the World War II won the Pulitzer Prize. The citation read: "for distinguished service as a cartoonist, as exemplified by the series entitled 'Up Front With Mauldin.'" Mauldin was the youngest person to be awarded the prize.

ASSIGNMENT

1. Click on and look at some of Mauldin's cartoons shown on the left side.
2. Pick out one that you find interesting.
3. Copy and print out the cartoon that you will include on your poster.
4. Write a brief analysis of the cartoon:

   1. Describe the action taking place in the cartoon.
   2. In your own words, explain how the words in the cartoon explain or clarify the symbols.
   3. What techniques or devices does the cartoonist use? Symbolism? Ridicule? Caricature? Metaphor? Satire? Puns? Other?
   4. In your own words, explain the message of the cartoon.
   5. Which words or phrases in the cartoon appear to be the most significant? Why do you think so?

SMITHSONIAN WORLD WAR II WEBSITE

Click on: http://americanhistory.si.edu/militaryhistory/exhibition/flash.html

ASSIGNMENT

1. On the World War II home page, read the introduction and then click "Begin."
2. On the next page, click on "Play Movie." As you watch the 2-minute movie, jot down 3 things that you learned. Use the pause button to stop the movie if you need to.

3. Then click on "Enter Exhibit."
4. Note at the top that there are 11 sections. Click on one of them.
5. Explore the "Artifacts" along the bottom of the page.
6. Choose one slideshow (ones with titles) and one artifact (ones with pictures).
7. Write a description of what you learned and what you saw.

STATION 6: WORLD WAR II—VIDEO

Teacher Instructions

MATERIALS NEEDED

World War II: Cause and Effect. Iconographic, 2000. 60 minutes. $29.95.

STATION CONSTRUCTION

The specific video that goes with the worksheets included here is *World War II: Cause and Effect,* available from the Library Video Company. Because it is 60 minutes long, it lends itself to being shown in two 30-minute segments. The first segment should be shown in the classroom before the class comes to the library for the stations. It highlights the build-up to and beginnings of war in Europe. The second segment begins with the bombing of Pearl Harbor and highlights the U.S. role in the war, which is the primary focus of this World War II station unit. If desired, another World War II video could be shown. Be sure to choose a video that surveys the whole war or choose one that highlights an aspect of the war that was not covered in depth in the classroom.

To help the students better watch the video and not be distracted by spelling and writing answers, a list of the answers in alphabetical order is given next to the questions. In this way students can jot down the correct letter and fill in the full answer after the video is over.

WORLD WAR II: CAUSE AND EFFECT—PART 1

As you watch the video, write down the *letter* of the correct answer to the fill-in-the-blank questions. The questions are in the same order as the video and the answers are in alphabetical order. After the video, go back and completely fill in the correctly spelled answers.

A. Atlantic Charter

B. Barbarossa

C. Battle of Britain

D. Benito Mussolini

E. Berlin

F. blitz

G. Dunkirk

H. Fuhrer

I. isolationism

J. Japan

K. Joseph Stalin

L. Kristallnacht

M. League of Nations

N. Lend-Lease

O. London

1. _____ was called "The war to end all wars."

2. A new postwar Europe was created with the Treaty of _____.

3. The _____ was formed to settle international disputes.

4. The U.S. Senate wished to return to an age of _____ _____, so it never joined the League of Nations.

5. The German party known as the _____ was led by Adolph Hitler.

6. Hitler's autobiography was called _____, or *My Struggle,* which outlined his plans for Germany.

7. After the German Reichstag fire, Hitler assumed both the presidency and chancellorship under the new title: _____.

8. The Nazis destroyed Jewish businesses and synagogues during _____, or "Night of Broken Glass."

9. Italy's leader was named _____.

10. British Prime Minister _____ tried to appease Hitler by giving him the Sudetenland.

11. Chamberlain claimed to have secured "_____."

12. Hitler signed a nonaggression pact with the Soviet dictator, _____.

13. A 250-mile long series of heavily defended fortifications along the border between France and Germany was known as the _____.

14. The new British Prime Minister, _____, exclaimed, "Victory at all costs....For without victory, there is no survival."

15. In the evacuation of _____, 340,000 allied troops were saved.

P. Maginot Line

Q. *Mein Kampf*

R. Nazis

S. Neville Chamber-
    lain

T. peace in our time

U. radar

V. Sea Lion

W. Versailles

X. Vichy

Y. Winston Churchill

Z. winter

AA. World War I

16. After the Nazis took Paris, the French government was led by Pétain, from the city of _____ in southern France.

17. Hitler and his generals planned the invasion of Great Britain and named it Operation _____.

18. The German air force, the Luftwaffe, was larger than the British Royal Air Force (RAF), but the British had a new invention called _____.

19. The _____ had some of the fiercest "dog-fights" (airplane battles) in history.

20. The British bombed the German capital of _____, so the Germans retaliated by bombing the British capital of _____ in an attack called the _____.

21. In September 1940, _____ joined the Axis powers of Germany and Italy.

22. In his last fireside chat of 1940, President Roosevelt told the people that the United States must be "the great arsenal of democracy." On March 11, 1941 this resulted in the _____ Act.

23. Hitler's most ambitious project of the war was Operation _____, the invasion of the Soviet Union.

24. The drive to Moscow by the Nazis was stopped by the ferocious Russian fighters and the Russian _____.

25. On August 11, 1941, Churchill and Roosevelt met and signed a joint declaration of war aims called the _____.

World War II—Video

WORLD WAR II: CAUSE AND EFFECT—PART 1

ANSWER SHEET

As you watch the video, write down the *letter* of the correct answer to the fill-in-the-blank questions. The questions are in the same order as the video and the answers are in alphabetical order. After the video, go back and completely fill in the correctly spelled answers.

1. *World War I* was called "The war to end all wars."
2. A new postwar Europe was created with the Treaty of *Versailles.*
3. The *League of Nations* was formed to settle international disputes.
4. The U.S. Senate wished to return to an age of *isolationism,* so it never joined the League of Nations.
5. The German party known as the *Nazis* was led by Adolph Hitler.
6. Hitler's autobiography was called *Mein Kampf,* or *My Struggle,* which outlined his plans for Germany.
7. After the German Reichstag fire, Hitler assumed both the presidency and chancellorship under the new title: *Fuhrer.*
8. The Nazis destroyed Jewish businesses and synagogues during *Kristallnacht,* or "Night of Broken Glass."
9. Italy's leader was named *Benito Mussolini.*
10. British Prime Minister *Neville Chamberlin* tried to appease Hitler by giving him the Sudetenland.
11. Chamberlain claimed to have secured *"peace in our time."*
12. Hitler signed a nonaggression pact with the Soviet dictator, *Joseph Stalin.*
13. A 250-mile long series of heavily defended fortifications along the border between France and Germany was known as the *Maginot Line.*
14. The new British Prime Minister, *Winston Churchill,* exclaimed "Victory at all costs. . . . For without victory, there is no survival."
15. In the evacuation of *Dunkirk,* 340,000 allied troops were saved.
16. After the Nazis took Paris, the French government was led by Pétain, from the city of *Vichy* in southern France.
17. Hitler and his generals planned the invasion of Great Britain and named it Operation *Sea Lion.*
18. The German air force, the Luftwaffe, was larger than the British Royal Air Force (RAF), but the British had a new invention called *radar.*
19. The *Battle of Britain* had some of the fiercest "dog-fights" (airplane battles) in history.
20. The British bombed the German capital of *Berlin,* so the Germans retaliated by bombing the British capital of *London* in an attack called the *blitz.*
21. In September 1940, *Japan* joined the Axis powers of Germany and Italy.
22. In his last fireside chat of 1940, President Roosevelt told the people that the United States must be "the great arsenal of democracy." On March 11, 1941 this resulted in the *Lend-Lease* Act.
23. Hitler's most ambitious project of the war was Operation *Barbarossa,* the invasion of the Soviet Union.

24. The drive to Moscow by the Nazis was stopped by the ferocious Russian fighters and the Russian *winter*.

25. On August 11, 1941, Churchill and Roosevelt met and signed a joint declaration of war aims called the *Atlantic Charter*.

WORLD WAR II: CAUSE AND EFFECT—PART 2

As you watch the video, write down the *letter* of the correct answer to the fill-in-the-blank questions. The questions are in the same order as the video and the answers are in alphabetical order. After the video, go back and completely fill in the correctly spelled answers.

A. Bataan

1. _____ was the Japanese prime minister who called for the attack on Pearl Harbor.

B. Battle of the Bulge

2. President Roosevelt called Dec. 7, 1941, "A date which will live in _____."

C. Bernard Montgomery

3. The commander of the U.S. forces in the Philippines was General _____. When he left, he vowed, "I shall return."

D. Cold War

4. The Japanese marched 76,000 prisoners over 60 miles in the heat. More than 22,000 prisoners died in the _____ Death March.

E. D-Day

5. Chester Nimitz was commander of the U.S. Pacific fleet, which launched a surprise attack at _____.

F. Douglas MacArthur

6. The German leader of the Africa Korps was _____, nicknamed the "Desert Fox."

G. Dwight D. Eisenhower

7. British Prime Minister Winston Churchill chose a new commander in North Africa named General _____.

H. George S. Patton

8. In the Battle of _____, 200,000 Russians and 140,000 Germans lost their lives in the defeat of the Nazis.

I. Harry S Truman

9. The Allies attacked Sicily led by General Montgomery and American General _____.

J. Hideki Tojo

10. The Big 3—Churchill, Stalin, and Roosevelt—discussed "Operation Overload" and chose General _____ to lead it.

K. Hiroshima

11. On June 6, 1944, _____, the largest amphibious attack in history was launched at Normandy.

L. Holocaust

12. The Allies reconquered France and entered its capital of _____, while the Soviets entered Poland and its capital of _____.

M. infamy

13. General MacArthur returned to the Philippines announcing, "I have returned" and fought the largest naval battle in history at _____.

N. Iron Curtain

14. Japanese suicide pilots were called _____.

O. Irwin Rommel

15. Hitler's final attempt to win the war occurred in the Ardennes Forest and resulted in a 30-mile Allied retreat know as the _____.

P. Iwo Jima

Q. Kamikaze

R. Leyte Gulf

S. Midway

T. Okinawa

U. Paris

V. Rhine

W. Stalingrad

X. V-E Day

Y. Warsaw

Z. Yalta

16. In 1945 the Big Three met at _____ and made plans for postwar Europe.

17. The Allied troops poured into Germany by crossing the _____ River.

18. When Franklin D. Roosevelt (FDR) died, he was succeeded by _____.

19. "Victory in Europe," May 8, 1945, was called _____ Day.

20. _____ island saw some of the bloodiest fighting of the war, but the Americans raised the flag in victory, despite losing 6,000 men.

21. In the battle at _____ over 12,000 Americans and more than 100,000 Japanese lost their lives.

22. On August 6, 1945, the *Enola Gay* dropped the first atomic bomb on the Japanese city of _____.

23. More than six million Jews perished in the Nazi concentration camps using Hitler's "Final Solution." It became known as the _____.

24. Winston Churchill described the Soviet Union's Communist influence as an _____ descending on Europe.

25. The resulting conflict became known as the _____.

STATION 6: WORLD WAR II—VIDEO

WORLD WAR II: CAUSE AND EFFECT—PART 2

ANSWER SHEET

As you watch the video, write down the *letter* of the correct answer to the fill-in-the-blank questions. The questions are in the same order as the video and the answers are in alphabetical order. After the video, go back and completely fill in the correctly spelled answers.

1. *Hideki Tojo* was the Japanese prime minister who called for the attack on Pearl Harbor.
2. President Roosevelt called Dec. 7, 1941, "A date which will live in *infamy*."
3. The commander of the U.S. forces in the Philippines was General *Douglas MacArthur*. When he left, he vowed, "I shall return."
4. The Japanese marched 76,000 prisoners over 60 miles in the heat. More than 22,000 prisoners died in the *Bataan* Death March.
5. Chester Nimitz was commander of the U.S. Pacific Fleet, which launched a surprise attack at *Midway*.
6. The German leader of the Africa Korps was *Irwin Rommel*, nicknamed the "Desert Fox."
7. British Prime Minister Winston Churchill chose a new commander in North Africa named General *Bernard Montgomery*.
8. In the Battle of *Stalingrad*, 200,000 Russians and 140,000 Germans lost their lives in the defeat of the Nazis.
9. The Allies attacked Sicily led by General Montgomery and American General *George S. Patton*.
10. The Big 3—Churchill, Stalin, and Roosevelt—discussed "Operation Overload" and chose General *Dwight D. Eisenhower* to lead it.
11. On June 6, 1944, *D-Day*, the largest amphibious attack in history, was launched at Normandy.
12. The Allies reconquered France and entered its capital of *Paris*, while the Soviets entered Poland and its capital of *Warsaw*.
13. General MacArthur returned to the Philippines announcing, "I have returned" and fought the largest naval battle in history at *Leyete Gulf*.
14. Japanese suicide pilots were called *kamikaze*.
15. Hitler's final attempt to win the war occurred in the Ardennes Forest and resulted in a 30-mile Allied retreat know as the *Battle of the Bulge*.
16. In 1945 the Big Three met at *Yalta* and made plans for postwar Europe.
17. The Allied troops poured into Germany by crossing the *Rhine* River.
18. When Franklin D. Roosevelt (FDR) died, he was succeeded by *Harry S Truman*.
19. "Victory in Europe," May 8, 1945, was called *V-E* Day.
20. *Iwo Jima* island saw some of the bloodiest fighting of the war, but the Americans raised the flag in victory, despite losing 6,000 men.

21. In the battle at *Okinawa* over 12,000 Americans and more than 100,000 Japanese lost their lives.
22. On August 6, 1945, the *Enola Gay* dropped the first atomic bomb on the Japanese city of *Hiroshima*.
23. More than six million Jews perished in the Nazi concentration camps using Hitler's "Final Solution." It became known as the *Holocaust*.
24. Winston Churchill described the Soviet Union's Communist influence as an *Iron Curtain* descending on Europe.
25. The resulting conflict became known as the *Cold War*.

CHAPTER 3

Holocaust Stations

The station unit on the Holocaust originated when an English teacher wanted to develop a background unit for his students who were going to read *Anne Frank: Diary of a Young Girl*. The original unit had four stations: Hyperstudio slides, Research, Hangman/Rose Blanche, and Eyewitness Accounts. Over the years, two other stations have been added: Video and Poetry. Teachers have selected some or all of the stations for their classes depending on the level of the class and the amount of time available to do the unit. The unit has also been used many times by classes preparing to read *Night* by Elie Wiesel, and by history classes studying the Holocaust and World War II.

Station one involves watching a slide show during which the students answer accompanying questions. The original show was made using Hyperstudio, but a similar presentation can be made using PowerPoint. However, there are now Holocaust presentations available on the Internet. The website: http://222.historyplace.com has a photo essay on the Holocaust that works really well. A set of questions and answers to use with it is included in this unit.

At the second station, students do research using both books and the Internet to find information about various Holocaust-related topics. They use the information they find to create a poster, write a report, and make a presentation to the class.

Students read and listen to the poem, "The Hangman," and the picture book, *Rose Blanche*, by Roberto Innocenti, at station three. There have been many excellent picture books related to the Holocaust published in the last few years and any of these could be used. Students are able to listen to the readings on headsets as they follow along in the book and on the handout. They then respond to short-answer questions from the readings.

At station four, students read excerpts from first-hand accounts of people involved in the Holocaust. Students work in pairs to discuss the articles and then develop a graphic illustrating what they considered important.

Station five requires the students to read poems written by Holocaust survivors. They then analyze the poems and react to what they read.

At station six, students watch the video, *The Holocaust: In Memory of Millions* and take notes. They then write an essay reflecting what they learned and what they felt.

TEACHER INSTRUCTIONS

Before the class comes to the library, the classroom teacher needs to do two things. First, divide the students into six groups, numbered one through six. The students will begin at the station that matches their number and then rotate in order through the stations. Second, the teacher should assign or have the students choose which of the topics they will be researching.

Name_____

Teacher_____

Date_____ Per._____

Group Number_____

HOLOCAUST NOTEBOOK

Your notebook will include the following, clearly labeled, in order given.

Your Points	Possible Points		
_____	20	**Station 1:**	**Holocaust Internet Photo Essay** - Complete student assignment sheet
_____	50	**Station 2:**	**Research Assignment** - Report and presentation
_____	20	**Station 3:**	**Hangman/Rose Blanche** - Listen to tape of poem and picture book - Complete student assignment sheet
_____	20	**Station 4:**	**Eyewitness Accounts** - Primary sources - Notes and graphic of major ideas with partner
_____	20	**Station 5:**	**Poetry** - Read the 3 poems - Write essay
_____	20	**Station 6:**	**Video/Art** - Watch video - Write essay
_____	150	**Total Points**	
_____		**Your Grade**	

STATION 1: HOLOCAUST INTERNET PHOTO ESSAY

Teacher Instructions

STATION CONSTRUCTION

Make a link on the library's website for http://www.historyplace.com/.

STATION 1: HOLOCAUST INTERNET PHOTO ESSAY

ASSIGNMENT

1. Go to Internet at: http://www.historyplace.com/.
2. Scroll down about 3/4 of the page to the heading below:

Nazi Germany/World War II

• Special Topics

Auschwitz Today: Photo Essay

3. Click on it and read the introduction.
4. Click on "FIRST PHOTO" and look at the 20 pictures and captions. As you read the introduction and all the captions, find the answers to the questions below. (They are in order starting with the introduction.)

   1. How many total people were killed at Auschwitz? _____
   2. What does "Arbeit Macht Frei" mean in English? _____
   3. What happened at the Wall of Death? _____
   4. When new arrivals were separated, those chosen for work went in one direction, and the remainder, falsely told they were going to take disinfecting baths and have a warm meal, were moved in procession to the _____.
   5. What were the three main parts of the crematory? _____ and _____ and the _____ with ovens on the ground floor.
   6. What was the main bug that needed to be exterminated? _____
   7. What was the name of the cyanide gas pellet used to kill both people and vermin? _____
   8. How many inmates were housed in each of the barracks that had originally been designed as horse stables? _____
   9. How many people slept at each bunk level? _____
   10. What were two common infections suffered by the inmates because of the unsanitary conditions? _____

STATION 1: HOLOCAUST INTERNET PHOTO ESSAY

ANSWERS TO INTERNET QUESTIONS

1. How many total people were killed at Auschwitz? *1.6 million*
2. What does "Arbeit Macht Frei" mean in English? *Work Makes Free*
3. What happened at the Wall of Death? *20,000 inmates were shot from behind while standing naked.*
4. When new arrivals were separated, those chosen for work went in one direction, the remainder, falsely told they were going to take disinfecting baths and have a warm meal, were moved in procession to the *gas chambers.*
5. What were the three main parts of the crematory? *Underground dressing room* and *gas chamber* and the *furnace room* with ovens on the ground floor.
6. What was the main bug that needed to be exterminated? *Lice*
7. What was the name of the cyanide gas pellet used to kill both people and vermin? *Zyklon B*
8. How many inmates were housed in each of the barracks that had originally been designed as horse stables? *800 or more*
9. How many people slept at each bunk level? *6 to 8*
10. What were two common infections suffered by the inmates because of the unsanitary conditions? *typhus and dysentery*

STATION 2: HOLOCAUST RESEARCH

Teacher Instructions

MATERIALS NEEDED

1.   Books with information on the Holocaust topics.

   These would include reference and regular books specifically on the Holocaust and
      books on World War II that include information on the Holocaust.
   Some suggested titles:
   Baumel, Judith. *The Holocaust Encyclopedia.* New Haven, Conn.: Yale University
      Press, 2001. 765p. $75. 0–300–08432–3.
   Harran, Marilyn, ed. *The Holocaust Chronicle: A History in Word and Pictures.*
      Lincolnwood, Ill.: Publications International, Ltd., 2000. 768p. $31. 0–7853–
      2963–3.
   Lawton, Clive. *The Story of the Holocaust.* New York: Franklin Watts, 1999. 48p.
      $27. 0–531–14524–7.
   Meltzer, Milton. *Never to Forget: The Jews of the Holocaust.* New York: Harper and
      Row, 1976. 217p. op. 0–06–024174–8.
   Rozette, Robert, ed. *Encyclopedia of the Holocaust.* New York: Facts on File, 2000.
      528p. op. 0–8160–4333–7.

2.   Note papers
3.   Source pages with two books and two Internet sites, see Appendix 4.

STATION CONSTRUCTION

1.   Put the books that have been pulled from the shelves on a book cart next to where
      the station is located. (Hint: Locating the station near the copier makes copying
      convenient and quicker.)
2.   Have the note papers as well as additional source pages at the station.

STATION 2: HOLOCAUST RESEARCH

ASSIGNMENT

In order to better understand what happened during the Holocaust, we will be researching a number of Holocaust-related topics. Each of you will write a one-page paper about your topic. You will also make a poster or some type of visual that you will use to briefly (2–3 minutes) tell the class about your topic.

TOPICS

1. Allies/Axis
2. Anti-Semitism
3. Aryan Race
4. Auschwitz
5. Bergen-Belsen
6. Buchenwald
7. Dachau
8. Death Marches
9. Death Squads
10. Deportations
11. Eichmann, Adolph
12. Final Solution
13. Gas Chambers
14. Genocide
15. Gestapo
16. Goebbels, Joseph
17. Goering, Hermann
18. Himmler, Heinrich
19. Hitler Youth
20. Holocaust Memorial
21. Jewish Resistance
22. Krakow Ghetto
23. Kristallnacht
24. Liberation
25. *Mein Kampf*
26. Mengle, Josef
27. Nazis
28. Nuremberg Laws
29. Olympics (Berlin, 1936)
30. Partisans
31. Propaganda
32. Ravensbruck
33. SS
34. Schindler, Oskar
35. Star of David
36. Treblinka
37. Warsaw Ghetto
38. Wiesenthal, Simon
39. Zyklon B

RESEARCH STEPS

1. Find and use at least one book and one Internet source on your topic. Minimum of:

   - Six notes from the book
   - Six notes from Internet source

2. Record bibliographic information for each source.
3. Use the library website or search engines for Internet sources.

From *Collaborative Library Research Projects: Inquiry that Stimulates the Senses* by John D. Volkman. Westport, CT: Libraries Unlimited. Copyright © 2008.

POSTER REQUIREMENTS

1. Size: 28" × 22"
2. Contents:

   • Photos, drawings, maps of pertinent people, events, places
   • Appropriate typed captions in your own words for each picture
   • Short, word-processed information describing topic.

3. Your name in the lower right-hand corner of the front side.
4. On back side write two questions that other students should be able to answer after reading your poster.

GRADING

1.	One-page article	15 points	_____
2.	Note cards/bibliography	(10 points)	
	• Sources all in one list alphabetically	1 point	_____
	• Book sources in proper form	3 points	_____
	• Internet sources in proper form	3 points	_____
	• Minimum of 12 note papers	3 points	_____
3.	Poster	10 points	_____
4.	Oral Presentation	15 points	_____
5.	Total	50 points	_____

STATION 3: "THE HANGMAN"/*ROSE BLANCHE*

Teacher Instructions

MATERIALS NEEDED

1. Copies of the poem, "The Hangman," by Maurice Ogden, and Martin Niemoeller's poem, "First"
2. "They Came…" available on the Internet at sites such as these: http://academic. kellogg.edu/mandel/ConroyAftermath.htm http://edhelper.com/poetry/The_ Hangman_by_Maurice_Ogden.htm
3. Copies of the picture book, *Rose Blanche*. (Innocenti, Roberto. *Rose Blanche*. San Diego, Calif.: Harcourt Brace, 1996. 32p. 0–15–200917–5. It is out of print, but used copies are available from Amazon.)
4. Listening stations with headsets and CD or cassette player
5. CD player or cassette tape recorder
6. Computer with CD burner

STATION CONSTRUCTION

1. Copy and print out about 6–8 copies of the two poems. Laminate the sheets.
2. Obtain at least one copy of *Rose Blanche*. (Multiple copies are better.) One of the many other picture books on the Holocaust could be used, if preferred.
3. Record readings of the poems and of the picture book, either on a CD or cassette tape. Get one of your speech or drama students or someone else with dramatic ability to make the recording.

STATION 3: "THE HANGMAN"/*ROSE BLANCHE*

Listen to the story on CD/tape and follow along on the laminated sheet. Then go back and answer the questions as you take a closer look at the poem.

1. Briefly summarize what happens in the poem. (Briefly retell the story.)
2. What colors are used in the poem and what might these colors symbolize?
3. What do the gallows represent?
4. Why do the gallows continue to grow?
5. What is it "feeding on" or using to build and strengthen itself?
6. Who or what does the hangman represent? (Who or what might he symbolize?)
7. At the end of the poem, what does the hangman say to the narrator?
8. What happens to the narrator of the story and why does this happen?
9. What lesson in life is Maurice Ogden, the poet, trying to convey in "The Hangman"?
10. What are your reactions to Holocaust survivor Martin Niemoeller's poem?

Jews Captured

ROSE BLANCHE

Listen to the story on CD/tape and follow along in the book. Then go back and answer the questions as you take a closer look at the story and the pictures.

1. When Rose walks by the river, what else does she see beside branches and broken toys?
2. What does the mayor wear on his arm?
3. At what was Rose looking when she saw prisoners behind a barbed-wire fence?
4. What was Rose doing with her food?
5. What happened to Rose in the end?
6. How would you have felt if you were a child of Rose's age living as she did during the war?
7. Why did the author write this children's book? (In other words, explain the author's purpose and what he was trying to communicate.)
8. How do you think most children would react to this story? Describe their feelings and their thoughts/ideas. Would you read this story to your child? At what age?

From *Collaborative Library Research Projects: Inquiry that Stimulates the Senses* by John D. Volkman. Westport, CT: Libraries Unlimited. Copyright © 2008.

STATION 4: HOLOCAUST GRAPHIC

Teacher Instructions

MATERIALS NEEDED

Choose excerpts from 6–8 Holocaust sources that contain first-hand accounts. There are an endless number of sources available both in books and on the Internet. The books listed below are excellent sources of first-hand accounts of Holocaust survivors.

- Meltzer, Milton. *Never to Forget: The Jews of the Holocaust.* New York: Harper & Row, 1976.
- Rochman, Hazel, and Darlene Z. McCampbell. *Bearing Witness.* New York: Orchard Books, 1995.
- Ten Boom, Corrie. *The Hiding Place.* New York: Bantam, 1971.
- *Voices of the Holocaust.* Logan, Utah: Perfection Learning, 2000.
- Wiesel, Elie. *Night.* New York: Bantam, 1960.

STATION CONSTRUCTION

1. Peruse your sources and pick out excerpts that are about 1 1/2 to 1 3/4 pages long.
2. Choose 6–8 excerpts and copy them on 8 1/2" × 11" paper.
3. Make three copies of each excerpt that you choose.
4. Number each set of three with the same number.
5. Laminate these sheets.

STATION 4: HOLOCAUST GRAPHIC

1. Work together with a partner.
2. Each pair gets *1* set of the laminated sheets. (Pick only **1** set from sets 1–8, not all 8.)
3. Both of you will read the *same* article.
4. Take notes on the main ideas of the article/letters.
5. Draw a single page picture/graphic using colored pencils or markers.
6. Make a second copy of the picture so that you each have one to turn in.

REQUIREMENTS FOR GRAPHIC

1. In your picture/graphic use *color, symbols, words,* and *shapes* to convey your ideas.
2. At the top of the picture, put a *Title* for it.
3. Underneath your drawing, write a couple of sentences summarizing what you are showing in it. You may include short and meaningful quotations from the selection. Choose phrases that communicate an idea and are not long.

From *Collaborative Library Research Projects: Inquiry that Stimulates the Senses* by John D. Volkman. Westport, CT: Libraries Unlimited. Copyright © 2008.

STATION 5: HOLOCAUST POETRY

Teacher Instructions

MATERIALS NEEDED

Poems that deal with the Holocaust.

Poems can be found on the Internet as well as in books. The books listed below are two excellent ones:

- Sachs, Nelly. *O the Chimneys.* New York: Farrar, Straus and Giroux, 1967. 387p. op. 0–374–22380–7.
- Schiff, Hilda, comp. *Holocaust Poetry.* New York: St. Martin's Griffin, 1996. 256p. $14.95. 0–312–13086–4.

STATION CONSTRUCTION

1. Choose three poems that deal with the Holocaust. The three listed below are good choices:

    • "Never Shall I Forget," by Elie Wiesel
    • "O the Chimneys," by Nelly Sachs
    • "After Auschwitz," anonymous

2. Copy these poems onto a single sheet of paper that will be included in the students' packets.

STATION 5: HOLOCAUST POETRY

1. Read each of the three poems.
2. Take notes on the poems, keeping in mind the bulleted list below.
3. Write 2–3 paragraphs that include the following information:

  - Include five images in the poems that illustrated to you the horrors of the Holocaust.
  - Briefly summarize each of the poems and your reaction to them.
  - How did each of the poets view the Holocaust?
  - What were some of the common themes or ideas in the poems?

From *Collaborative Library Research Projects: Inquiry that Stimulates the Senses* by John D. Volkman. Westport, CT: Libraries Unlimited. Copyright © 2008.

STATION 6: HOLOCAUST VIDEO

Teacher Instructions

MATERIALS NEEDED

The Holocaust: In Memory of Millions. Discovery Channel, 1994. op. 60 minutes. (The video is still available on Amazon; there are other Holocaust videos that could be used, too.)

STATION CONSTRUCTION

1. Watch the video.
2. Edit and select the best 25–27 minutes so that you have a segment that will fit into the station time schedule.

STATION 6: THE HOLOCAUST: VIDEO

The narrator, Walter Cronkite, says: "For those unable to find refuge from the persecutions of Nazi Germany…there was another way out: a one-way trip to one of the thousands of slave-labor, concentration camps, and death camps established by the Nazis. Millions made that journey."

ASSIGNMENT

1. Watch the video about the Holocaust. As you watch, consider the many images suggested in it.
2. Jot down images that you observe and take notes on ones that strike you the most.
3. Write a short (250–300 words) essay or poem about it.

   • In the essay or poem reflect on what happened to the victims of the Holocaust.
   • Listen for the statements below from Elie Wiesel. Apply them in your essay or poem.

      • "To forget is to kill them again. Lack of knowledge invites shame."
      • "How could killers kill and go on living?"
      • "Memory is a shield. If I don't remember, then what weapon do I have? It is a powerful weapon."

   To aid your viewing, some of the images in the video are listed below:

- Trains
- Hold sun back
- Cattle cars
- No food, water
- Bucket for sanitation
- Never saw father again
- Age of 16—all alone
- No hair
- Recycled clothes
- No name, just a number
- Not a person
- Horrible sleeping quarters
- Numb
- Lice
- Roll-call
- Pits
- Burn bodies
- Pile of shoes
- Chimneys
- Crematoriums
- Gas chambers

From *Collaborative Library Research Projects: Inquiry that Stimulates the Senses* by John D. Volkman. Westport, CT: Libraries Unlimited. Copyright © 2008.

CHAPTER 4

To Kill a Mockingbird Stations

To Kill a Mockingbird by Harper Lee (New York: Harper Collins, 1960) is an American classic that is read and studied by students across the United States. Most students' lives today are far removed from the kind of prejudice and segregation that existed in this country in the first half of the twentieth century. The six-station unit on *To Kill a Mockingbird* was developed to help students better understand these themes of prejudice and segregation that are reflected in the book. The stations acquaint students with the emotions and feelings of that time period as well give them historical background on segregation, racial hatred, and the black experience in America.

The six stations include a video, a computer assignment, a music station, a contemporary account/graphic station, a poetry station, and a readings station. For the video station, the video, *A Time for Justice: America's Civil Rights Movement,* is perfect. It is available free from Tolerance.org, is 38 minutes long, and comes with a 108-page booklet, *Free at Last: A History of the Civil Rights Movement and Those Who Died in the Struggle.* The booklet includes two-page profiles of 40 people who gave their lives in the Civil Rights Movement. These profiles are perfect for the Contemporary Accounts used in station four.

The computer station provides a link to seeing, hearing, and learning about a mockingbird. It also has the students look up key words using electronic dictionaries, thesauri, and quotation sources. The music station has the students listen to a variety of jazz and blues songs and react to the songs and their lyrics.

The poetry station has the students listen to and read poems by black poets. They then answer a number of questions about the poems. The readings station has three short readings. The first is the biblical account of Joseph and Potiphar's wife in Genesis 29:1–23, which served as a source for the novel's plot. The second is an article about the book *Black Like Me* (John Howard Griffin, New York: Houghton, Mifflin, 1960), which recounts the experiences of a white man masquerading as a black man in the deep South during the 1960s. The third is the picture book, *The Story of Ruby Bridges,* by Robert Coles (New York: Scholastic Press, 1995), which tells the story of the first black child to attend an all-white elementary school in Mississippi.

Janet Adams, the English teacher who helped to construct this unit on *To Kill a Mockingbird,* wrote the following about her experience:

> The *To Kill A Mockingbird* library unit designed by Mr. Volkman, library media specialist, and me was implemented as an introduction to the teaching of Harper Lee's classic novel. Taught at the eleventh grade in the American Literature curriculum, the unit sought to integrate information regarding the Civil Rights movement of the 1960s, current laws and attitudes pertaining to civil rights, and historic social developments in the South of the 1930s. Through multi-modal approaches, students tap into prior knowledge and extend their background through examining cultural, social, literary, and legal artifacts.
>
> Mr. Volkman and I met during the planning of the unit to share resources and ideas for optimizing students' academic backgrounds, and learning and motivational levels. We combined resources I had been using in the classroom with library media center resources in developing six stations. To heighten interest and to tap into multi-modal levels, we incorporated audio, visual, literary, and computer activities. Not only do students hear the music, the words, and the segregationist issues during the 1930s setting of the novel, they make connections between the ensuing years of political unrest and violence which resulted in the historic work of civil rights activists and the enactment of the Civil Rights Act of 1964. As we engage in the reading of the novel, students are better able to grasp the significance of the events within the narrative, and to understand the actions of the characters.
>
> This unit has been shared with other American Literature teachers in our department who have found the library media center partnership exciting. Of particular note is the fact that the unit remains a work in progress which can be refined and improved through sharing and further resource development. Overall, the media/classroom partnership weaves a rich and colorful tapestry of knowledge, experience, and understanding.

As a wrap-up of the unit, there is a video on You Tube that is very effective. It adds dramatic pictures and text to the Bob Dylan song "The Death of Emmitt Till." The video is available at http://www.youtube.com/watch?v=QjfGcRM35xg. It was put together by Oscar Hernandez, an award-winning teacher at my high school, and is very powerful in illustrating to students the kind of hatred and prejudice that African Americans generally, and Tom Robinson specifically, were subject to in pre-Civil Rights America. The video is 4:16 long and can be shown to the students on the last day in the library or in the classroom.

To Kill a Mockingbird Notebook Cover Sheet

Name _____

Teacher _____

Date _____ Period _____

Your notebook will include the following, clearly labeled, in the order given.

Your Points	Possible Points		
_____	15	**Station 1:**	**Video: "A Time for Justice"** ◆ **Complete worksheet**
_____	20	**Station 2:**	**Computer Assignment** ◆ **Go to websites; look up words** ◆ **Write**
_____	15	**Station 3:**	**Music** ◆ **Listen to tape of blues/jazz music of the era** ◆ **Complete student assignment sheet**
_____	15	**Station 4**	**Contemporary Accounts** ◆ **Read and react to cases** ◆ **Complete notes and graphic of major ideas with a partner**
_____	15	**Station 5:**	**Poetry** ◆ **Listen and read poems written by black poets** ◆ **Complete student assignment sheet**
_____	20	**Station 6:**	**Readings** ◆ **Read and react to book readings** ◆ **Write answers to questions**
_____	100	**Total Points**	
_____		**Your Grade**	

STATION 1: A TIME FOR JUSTICE

Teacher Instructions

MATERIALS NEEDED

A Time for Justice: America's Civil Rights Movement. The video is 38 minutes long and is available at no cost from Tolerance.org: http://www.tolerance.org/teach/resources/civil_rights_movement.jsp.

STATION CONSTRUCTION

1. Watch the video.
2. The video is 38 minutes long. If necessary to keep the station to about a half an hour, it can be stopped at 28 minutes, right after the march from Selma starts. The answer to the last fill-in comes right at the 28-minute mark. Another option is to edit out the section from 20:31 to 28:00. The section is dramatic but not as important to understanding *To Kill a Mockingbird* as the first 20 minutes. No questions are included for that section.

STATION 1: TIME FOR JUSTICE

As you watch the video, write down the *letter* of the correct answer to the fill-in-the-blank questions. The questions are in the same order as the video and the answers are in alphabetical order. After the video, go back and completely fill in the correctly spelled answers. Then use your answers below and what you saw and heard in the video to write out answers to the essay questions at the end.

A. 100

B. 700

C. anti-discrimination laws

D. back

E. boy

F. corner

G. eyes on the prize

H. freedom riders

I. Jim Crow

J. Ku Klux Klan

K. Martin Luther King

L. nigger

M. not guilty

N. right

O. Rosa Parks

P. school

1. By 1954, slavery had been dead for almost _____ years.

2. In the 1950s, the average income of blacks was $_____ per year.

3. The unjust treatment of blacks endured. The black man says that when you are "told something so long whether it's right or not, you begin to feel like it's _____."

4. After Emmett Till was murdered, the trial had a jury of _____ jurors.

5. The blacks were in a separate _____ of the courtroom.

6. The murderers admitted killing Emmett, but in an hour the verdict was _____.

7. In Montgomery, Alabama, _____ _____ refused to give up her seat on a bus to a white man.

8. Blacks had to sit in the _____ part of the bus.

9. The leader of the bus boycott was _____ _____ _____.

10. When the bus boycott occurred, the black man said, "I ain't getting on, 'til _____ _____ gets off."

11. In 1957 in Little Rock, Arkansas, nine black children were threatened when they tried to attend an all-white _____.

12. In order to integrate lunch counters, there were a series of _____.

13. In spite of being harassed and hit, the blacks would "Just sit there and keep their '_____.'"

14. In May 1961 two groups left from Washington by bus to draw attention to violations of the _____ _____ in interstate travel.

15. The riders on the buses were called _____ _____.

16. When Martin Luther King went to Birmingham, he was criticized for going too far, too fast. In reply, he said, "When you have seen hate-filled policemen kick and kill black brothers and sisters, your first name becomes _____ and your middle name becomes _____, however, old you are,…then you will understand why we find it difficult to wait."

Q. sit-ins

17. The black girls in the Baptist Church were killed by a bomb set by the _____ _____ _____.

R. vote

18. Even though 50% of the eligible voters of Marion were black, only 1% were registered to vote. Thus, the march from Selma to Montgomery to present grievances to the governor was to get the right to _____.

S. white

Describe the feelings a black person may have felt during this time. Support your descriptions with examples of how you saw blacks being treated in the video.

What was the "prize" blacks kept their eyes on?

Describe some of the attitudes and actions of bigoted whites during that time.

Who/what was Jim Crow?

STATION 1: A TIME FOR JUSTICE

ANSWER SHEET

As you watch the video, fill in the blanks below. After the video, use the notes below and what you saw and heard to discuss and write about the questions at the bottom.

1. By 1954, slavery had been dead for almost *100* years.
2. In the 1950s, the average income of blacks was $*700* per year.
3. The unjust treatment of blacks endured. The black man says that when you are "told something so long whether it's right or not, you begin to feel like it's *right.*"
4. After Emmett Till was murdered, the trial had a jury of *white* jurors.
5. The blacks were in a separate *corner* of the courtroom.
6. The murderers admitted killing Emmett, but in an hour the verdict was *not guilty.*
7. In Montgomery, Alabama, *Rosa Parks* refused to give up her seat on a bus to a white man.
8. Blacks had to sit in the *back* part of the bus.
9. The leader of the bus boycott was *Martin Luther King.*
10. When the bus boycott occurred, the black man said, "I ain't getting on, 'til *Jim Crow* gets off."
11. In 1957 in Little Rock, Arkansas, nine black children were threatened when they tried to attend an all-white *school.*
12. In order to integrate lunch counters, there were a series of *sit-ins.*
13. In spite of being harassed and hit, the blacks would "Just sit there and keep their '*eyes on the prize.*'"
14. In May 1961 two groups left from Washington by bus to draw attention to violations of the *anti-discrimination laws* in interstate travel.
15. The riders on the buses were called *freedom riders.*
16. When Martin Luther King went to Birmingham, he was criticized for going too far, too fast. In reply, he said, "When you have seen hate-filled policemen kick and kill black brothers and sisters, your first name becomes *nigger* and your middle name becomes *boy,* however, old you are, . . . then you will understand why we find it difficult to wait."
17. The black girls in the Baptist Church were killed by a bomb set by the *Ku Klux Klan.*
18. Even though 50% of the eligible voters of Marion were black, only 1% were registered to vote. Thus, the march from Selma to Montgomery to present grievances to the governor was to get the right to *vote.*

STATION 2: COMPUTER WORDS

Teacher Instructions

STATION CONSTRUCTION

Make a link on the library's website for: http://www.holoweb.com/cannon/northergn.htm. Name it "Mockingbird."

Make a link on the library's website for http://www.refdesk.com/. Name it "Refdesk."

STATION 2: COMPUTER WORDS

THE MOCKINGBIRD

1. Click on the link for Mockingbird: http://www.holoweb.com/cannon/northergn. htm.
2. Look at the pictures and listen to mockingbird's song.
3. Skim the description to write down a couple things you learned about the mockingbird.
4. How many songs can it sing? _____ What is an example of a sound it can mimic? _____

WORD SEARCH ON THE COMPUTER

Pick out one of the words listed below and look it up in the three sources below.

prejudice	fear
courage	hate
rape	freedom
justice	revenge
anger	sin
brave	truth

Word: _____

- Go to http://www.refdesk.com/.
- Scroll down the right side about 2/3 of the way until you see the yellow heading "Top Reference Tools."

Dictionary

Find the category "Dictionaries & Thesaurus" and click on "Your Dictionary." Type in your word. Copy down its *definition:*

Go back to "Dictionaries & Thesaurus."

Thesaurus

Click on "Thesaurus.com." Type in your word. Write down 3–5 synonyms and 3–5 antonyms for your word.

Synonyms:

Antonyms:

Quotation

Scroll down the "Top Reference Tools" column and go to the heading "Quotations" and click on "Bartlett's." Type in your word. Click on a quotation that contains your word. Then copy down the quotation and the name of the person who said it.

Quotation:

Author:

Use your word in a sentence that illustrates the meaning of the word.

Sentence:

Example: Book

Definition: A set of written, printed, or blank pages fastened along one side and encased between protective covers.

Synonyms: album, bestseller, bible, brochure, copy

Antonyms: discharge, let go, liberate, release, set free

Quotation: "Books, the children of the brain."

Author: Jonathan Swift

Sentence: I observed that the man in the glasses was a fast reader because of how quickly he turned the pages of the *book* he was reading.

STATION 3: JAZZ/BLUES SONGS

Teacher Instructions

MATERIALS NEEDED

1. CDs of jazz/blues songs that reflect pre-Civil Rights America such as:

    Armstrong, Louis. *The Definitive Collection.* Hip-O Records, 2006. $9.97.
    Fitzgerald, Ella. *Pure Ella: The Very Best of Ella Fitzgerald.* Verve, 1998. $13.98.
    Holiday, Billie. 20th Century Masters—The Millennium Collection: The Best of
        Billie Holiday. Hip-O Records, 2002. $11.98.
    The Nitty Gritty Dirt Band. *Greatest Hits.* Curb Records, 1990. $7.98.
    Waters, Ethel. *Ethel Waters 1935 to 1940.* Classics, 1998. $15.98.

2. Listening stations with headsets and CD player
3. Computer with CD burner
4. Websites with jazz/blues song lyrics

STATION CONSTRUCTION

Jazz/blues CDs are readily available in stores and online or by borrowing from yours or someone else's collection. Choose ones whose artists or lyrics reflect pre-Civil Rights America.

From the CDs, choose six to eight songs that total about 25 minutes. Burn them to a single CD. To make this station as enjoyable and straight-forward as possible for the students, simply have the students rate the songs and write brief reactions. The students can then write a paragraph or two summarizing their overall reactions to the most meaningful songs. The lyrics to most of the songs can be found by doing an Internet search for them at websites such as the ones below:

http://www.lyricsdepot.com/
http://www.lyricsfreak.com/
http://www.free-lyrics.org/

Copy and paste these lyrics onto a sheet that the students can use to follow the words of the songs. Pictures of the artists can also be found on the Internet and pasted on the lyrics page or on the assignment sheet. The lyrics can be included in the student packet or laminated sheets to be used at the station. You may also want to make another sheet that gives a brief biography of the artist. These sheets could be included in the packet or put on laminated sheets to be used at the station.

RATE A RECORD

Listen to the songs on the CD. On scale of 1 to 5 with 1 being lowest and 5 highest, rate each song on how much you liked the tune and how much the lyrics meant something to you. Also, give your reaction to each song.

1. Billie Holiday—Strange Fruit   Lyrics 1 2 3 4 5

What is the "strange fruit"?   Tune 1 2 3 4 5
Why do you think the writer made that comparison?
What contrasts do you find in these lyrics?
Reaction:

2. Billie Holiday—T'ain't Nobody's Bizness If I Do   Lyrics 1 2 3 4 5

What attitude does this song portray?   Tune 1 2 3 4 5
Reaction:

3. Ella Fitzgerald—A Tisket a Tasket   Lyrics 1 2 3 4 5

Reaction: Tune 1 2 3 4 5

4. Ella Fitzgerald—Take the 'A' Train   Lyrics 1 2 3 4 5

Reaction: Tune 1 2 3 4 5

5. Ethel Waters—Jeepers Creepers   Lyrics 1 2 3 4 5

Reaction: Tune 1 2 3 4 5

6. Nitty Gritty Dirt Band—Mr. Bojangles (Bill Robinson)   Lyrics 1 2 3 4 5

Describe what kind of life you think Bill Robinson had?   Tune 1 2 3 4 5
Reaction:

7. Louis Armstrong—I Got a Right to Sing the Blues   Lyrics 1 2 3 4 5

Reaction: Tune 1 2 3 4 5

STATION 4: CONTEMPORARY ACCOUNTS GRAPHIC

Teacher Instructions

MATERIALS NEEDED

Free at Last: A History of the Civil Rights Movement and Those Who Died in the Struggle. (This booklet is included with the video kit from Tolerance.org, which was described in station one.)

STATION CONSTRUCTION

1.   Peruse the 40 articles in the booklet on those who gave their lives for civil rights.
2.   Choose 6–8 that are two pages long and copy them back to back on 8 1/2" × 11" paper.
3.   Make three copies of each article that you choose.
4.   Number each set of three with the same number.
5.   Laminate these sheets.

STATION 4: CONTEMPORARY ACCOUNTS GRAPHIC

1. Work together with a partner.
2. Each pair gets *1* set of the laminated sheets (Pick only *1* set from sets 1–8, not all 8).
3. Both of you will read the *same* article.
4. Take notes on the main ideas of the article/letters.
5. Draw a single page picture/graphic using colored pencils or markers.
6. Make a second copy of the picture so that you each have one to turn in.

REQUIREMENTS FOR GRAPHIC

1. In your picture/graphic use *color, symbols, words,* and *shapes* to convey your ideas.
2. Include the answers to these questions on your graphic either in pictures or in writing:

   • What action triggered the murder or what reason was given for the murder?
   • What happened to the victim?
   • What happened to the murderer(s)?

3. Put a *title* for your picture/graphic at the top of it.
4. You may include short and meaningful quotations from the selection. Choose phrases that communicate an idea and are not long.

From *Collaborative Library Research Projects: Inquiry that Stimulates the Senses* by John D. Volkman. Westport, CT: Libraries Unlimited. Copyright © 2008.

STATION 5: BLACK POETRY

Teacher Instructions

MATERIALS NEEDED

1. Clinton, Catherine. *I, Too, Sing America: Three Centuries of African American Poetry.* Boston: Houghton Mifflin, 1998. 128p. $22. 0–395–89599–5.
2. Clinton, Catherine. *I, Too, Sing America: Three Centuries of African American Poetry.* Middletown, R.I.: Audio Bookshelf, 2000. 2 CDs. $28.95. 1–883332–57–5.
3. Listening stations with headsets and CD player
4. Computer with CD burner

STATION CONSTRUCTION

Use the audio CD of *I, Too, Sing America* and burn the following poems onto one CD:
Langston Hughes—"I, Too, Sing America"
W.E.B. DuBois—"The Song of the Smoke"
James Weldon Johnson—"Lift Ev'ry Voice and Sing"
Angelina Weld Grimke—"The Black Finger"
Claude McKay—"If We Must Die," "The White House"
Langston Hughes—"Harlem," Merry 'Go-Round," "Cross"

In the book, *I, Too, Sing America,* find the above poems and poets. Make copies of each of the poems and the one-page biography of each poet. Students can then follow along with the text of the poems as they listen. After they listen to the poems, they are to then go back and reread them as they write out a brief reaction to each one. Students should also read the biographies of each of the poets and write down a couple of interesting facts about the poet.

Make six to eight copies of the poems and biographies and put each set in a three-ring folder so that the students can easily use them at the station.

STATION 5: BLACK POETRY

1. Listen to the poems as you follow along with the words.
2. Listen to all the poems straight through.
3. Go back and reread the poems.
4. For each poem write a brief reaction, describing what you think it means and/or how it affected you.
5. Read the biographies of each of the poets.
6. For each poet, write down two interesting facts that you learned.

Langston Hughes—"I, Too, Sing America"
W.E.B. DuBois—"The Song of the Smoke"
James Weldon Johnson—"Lift Ev'ry Voice and Sing"
Angelina Weld Grimke—"The Black Finger"
Claude McKay—"If We Must Die," "The White House"
Langston Hughes—"Harlem," Merry 'Go-Round," "Cross"

STATION 6: READINGS

Teacher Instructions

MATERIALS NEEDED

- Coles, Robert. *The Story of Ruby Bridges.* New York: Scholastic, 1995. $16.95. 0–590–43967–7.
- Copy of *Genesis* 39:1–23
- Summary or information about *Black Like Me* by John Howard Griffin

STATION CONSTRUCTION

1. Obtain 2–4 copies of *The Story of Ruby Bridges.* It is available in paperback as well as hardcover so it is easy to get multiple copies.
2. Find *Genesis* 39:1–23 on the Internet. A good source is http://www.biblegateway. com/. You can use any version you like, but the Living Version is recommended because it is in contemporary language and easier for the students to understand.
3. Find information about *Black Like Me.*

    • Good article on the Internet:
    • Ladaga, Lili. "Black Like Me Celebrates 40th Anniversary." CNN.com. Jan. 11, 2001. http://archives.cnn.com/2001/books/news/01/11/black.like.me/.
    • There are many other articles available online including a good summary from Spark Notes: http://www.sparknotes.com/lit/blacklikeme/summary.html.

4. Make copies of the Bible passage and *Black Like Me* article to include in the student packets. Alternately, six to eight copies of these could be printed out and laminated and available at the station.
5. Have the copies of *The Story of Ruby Bridges* available at the station.

ASSIGNMENT

Follow the directions for each reading. Take notes on this paper or your own paper. Then use a word-processing program to write paragraphs answering the questions.

JOSEPH AND POTIPHAR'S WIFE

Read the biblical account of Joseph and Potiphar's wife found in Genesis 39:1–23, and in one to two paragraphs describe briefly what the story is about, including information about:

- Who was Joseph?

- How did Joseph react?
- What was his position?
- What happened to Joseph?
- What did Potiphar's wife do to Joseph?
- Was Joseph guilty?

BLACK LIKE ME

Read the article about *Black Like Me* and in one to two paragraphs briefly describe what John Howard Griffin did, including answers to these questions:

- How did he transform himself?
- What was an example of how he was treated as a black man?
- What was one reaction of the public to what he did?

RUBY BRIDGES

Read *The Story of Ruby Bridges* and in one to two paragraphs briefly describe what Ruby Bridges did, including answers to these questions:

- What was the significance of her going to a white school?
- What did white parents do?
- How did Ruby stay strong?

- What did her teacher do?
- What was the end result of what Ruby did?

CHAPTER 5

Animal Farm Stations

After having done the station units on the Holocaust and *To Kill a Mockingbird,* an English teacher inquired about developing a station unit as background to the reading of *Animal Farm.* The events surrounding the Russian Revolution form the basis of the book. Since familiarity with these events is vital in understanding the allegorical aspects of the story, the idea of creating stations to teach them was a natural. Four stations were developed: Video, Online Encyclopedia, Newspaper/Topics, and Biography Essay.

For station one, students watch a video that tells the story of the 1917 Russian Revolution and the takeover of the Communists. At the second station, students learn basic information about the Revolution by reading an online encyclopedia article about it and summarizing the most important aspects of it.

At station three, students are divided into groups of four or five and required to do research on five topics each. They then pool their information to report their information in the form of various newspaper-type blurbs. Station four consists of each student doing further research into the life of the person whose name they selected at station three. They then write a biographical essay about that person.

Name _____

Teacher _____

Date _____ Period _____

Animal Farm Notebook
Cover Sheet

Your notebook will include the following, clearly labeled, in the order given.

Your Points	Possible Points		
_____	**20**	**Station 1:**	**Video: Russian Revolution** ♦ **Fill in the blanks on the worksheet**
_____	**20**	**Station 2:**	**Computer/Graphic Organizer** ♦ **Find Russian Revolution in *World Book* online** ♦ **Fill-out graphic organizer**
_____	**50**	**Station 3:**	**Newspaper/Topics** ♦ **Do research on topics in book and on Internet** ♦ **Create newspaper to highlight information**
_____	**30**	**Station 4**	**Biography Essay** ♦ **Research person** ♦ **Take notes and record sources** ♦ **Write 2-page essay** ♦ **Bibliography in proper form**

_____ **140** **Total Points**

_____ **Your Grade**

From *Collaborative Library Research Projects: Inquiry that Stimulates the Senses* by John D. Volkman. Westport, CT: Libraries Unlimited. Copyright © 2008.

STATION 1: *ANIMAL FARM*—VIDEO

Teacher Instructions

MATERIALS NEEDED

The Russian Revolution. 23 minutes, 20 fill-in answers/points. Schlessinger Media, 2005. $39.95. The video is part of the *World Revolutions for Students* series.

STATION CONSTRUCTION

1. Watch the video.
2. Duplicate the question sheet.
3. Note: To help students better watch the video and not be distracted by spelling and writing answers, a list of the answers in alphabetical order is given near the questions. In this way students can jot down the correct letter and fill in the full answer after the video is over.

STATION 1: *ANIMAL FARM*—VIDEO

As you watch the video, write down the *letter* of the correct answer to the fill-in-the-blank answer. The questions are in the same order as the video and the answers are in alphabetical order. After the video, go back and completely fill-in the correctly spelled answers.

A. 1917

B. Abdicated

C. Bloody Sunday

D. Bourgeoisie

E. Collective

F. Great Terror

G. Gulags

H. Industrialization

I. Lenin

J. Marx

K. Moscow

L. Nicholas II

M. Proletariat

N. Quotas

O. Red Terror

P. Socialism

Q. Soviets

R. Stalin

S. Trotsky

T. White

1. In 1900 Russia was ruled by Tsar _____.

2. One of the privileged youth who turned revolutionary was Vladimir _____.

3. Many of Lenin's socialist beliefs were based on those of the German philosopher, Karl _____.

4. Those people working in the factories and getting low wages were known as the _____.

5. _____ were those who had enough money that they did not have to work with their hands.

6. _____ suggested taking property away from the rich and giving it to the government.

7. In October _____ Lenin and the Bolsheviks seized control of the government.

8. In 1905 a protest in St. Petersburg resulted in 200 workers being killed. It became known as _____ _____.

9. Elected Peoples' Councils were formed and known as _____. They gave an organized voice to the workers, peasants, and soldiers.

10. In February 1917 Tsar Nicholas II _____ (gave up) the throne and a new government was formed.

11. The Russian Civil War was between the Bolshevik Red Army and the _____ Army.

12. To cement their control, the Red Army embarked on a brutal campaign known as the _____.

13. The new country was named the Union of Soviet Socialist Republics (USSR) with _____ as its capital.

14. When Lenin died in 1924, the battle for control of the Soviet Union was between Josef _____ and Leon _____.

15. After Stalin won out over Trotsky in 1929, all of Russia's resources were dedicated to a new _____ drive.

16. Many peasants were herded onto vast _____ farms and forced to meet harsh production _____ set by the party.

17. Stalin launched the _____ of the 1930s in order to purge and arrest his enemies.

18. Enemies were sent to labor camps called _____ where millions were worked or starved to death.

STATION 1: *ANIMAL FARM*—VIDEO ANSWERS

As you watch the video, write down the *letter* of the correct answer to the fill-in-the-blank answer. The questions are in the same order as the video and the answers are in alphabetical order. After the video, go back and completely fill-in the correctly spelled answers.

A.	1917	1.	In 1900 Russia was ruled by Tsar *Nicholas II.*
B.	Abdicated	2.	One of the privileged youth who turned revolutionary was Vladimir *Lenin.*
C.	Bloody Sunday	3.	Many of Lenin's socialist beliefs were based on those of the German philosopher, Karl *Marx.*
D.	Bourgeoisie	4.	Those people working in the factories and getting low wages were known as the *proletariat.*
E.	Collective	5.	*Bourgeoisie* were those who had enough money that they did not have to work with their hands.
F.	Great Terror	6.	*Socialism* suggested taking property away from the rich and giving it to the government.
G.	Gulags	7.	In October *1917* Lenin and the Bolsheviks seized control of the government.
H.	Industrialization	8.	In 1905 a protest in St. Petersburg resulted in 200 workers being killed. It became known as *Bloody Sunday.*
I.	Lenin	9.	Elected Peoples' Councils were formed and known as *soviets.* They gave an organized voice to the workers, peasants, and soldiers.
J.	Marx	10.	In February 1917 Tsar Nicholas II *abdicated* (gave up) the throne and a new government was formed.
K.	Moscow	11.	The Russian Civil War was between the Bolshevik Red Army and the *White* Army.
L.	Nicholas II	12.	To cement their control, the Red Army embarked on a brutal campaign known as the *Red Terror.*
M.	Proletariat	13.	The new country was named the Union of Soviet Socialist Republics (USSR) with *Moscow* as its capital.
N.	Quotas	14.	When Lenin died in 1924, the battle for control of the Soviet Union was between Josef *Stalin* and Leon *Trotsky.*
O.	Red Terror	15.	After Stalin won out over Trotsky in 1929, all of Russia's resources were dedicated to a new *industrialization* drive.
P.	Socialism	16.	Many peasants were herded onto vast *collective* farms and forced to meet harsh production *quotas* set by the party.
Q.	Soviets	17.	Stalin launched the *Great Terror* of the 1930s in order to purge and arrest his enemies.
R.	Stalin	18.	Enemies were sent to labor camps called *gulags* where millions were worked or starved to death.
S.	Trotsky		
T.	White		

STATION 2: *ANIMAL FARM*—COMPUTER/GRAPHIC ORGANIZER

Teacher Instructions

MATERIALS NEEDED

1. *World Book Encyclopedia Online* or other Internet encyclopedia
2. Graphic Organizer forms

STATION CONSTRUCTION

If your library subscribes to an online encyclopedia such as *World Book, Grolier Online (Encyclopedia Americana)*, or *Britannica Online*, provide directions to the students on how to access the site. There are free encyclopedias such as *Columbia* and *Britannica Concise* available at http://www.refdesk.com/. Other encyclopedias can be located using a search engine.

English teachers use a variety of graphic organizers, so most of them would have ones that they have been using with their students. Many different types can easily be found by doing an online search for them. Pick one or more that work with historical events and people. The Schools of California Online Resources for Education has a dozen types that can be easily printed out and duplicated at: http://www.sdcoe.k12.ca.us/SCORE/actbank/sorganiz.htm.

STATION 2: *ANIMAL FARM*—COMPUTER/GRAPHIC ORGANIZER

1. Go to the *World Book Encyclopedia Online* or other online encyclopedia.
2. Type in "Russian Revolution of 1917."
3. Read the article.
4. Go back and pick out the most important events and people.
5. Click on the highlighted terms to get further information.
6. Use one or more graphic organizers to identify the essential people and events and explain their importance.

STATION 3: *ANIMAL FARM*—NEWSPAPER/TOPICS

Teacher Instructions

MATERIALS NEEDED

1. Books with information on the Russian Revolution topics:
   These would include reference and regular books specifically on the Russian Revolution; books on Russian history that cover that time period; and books that include information on the persons and events.
2. Note papers
3. Source pages with two books and two Internet sites, see Appendix 4.

STATION CONSTRUCTION

1. Provide examples of all the types of newspaper content that might be used.

   • Find an example of each of the "Types of Newspaper Content" listed below.
   • Make a one- or two-page collage of them with captions identifying them and photocopy the collage.
   • Make copies of the pages for the students to see as examples so that they know about the many types of newspaper content.

2. Divide the class into groups of five students; if there is an odd number, then use as many groups of four as necessary.
3. Put the books that have been pulled from the shelves on a book cart next to where the station is located. (Hint: Locating the station near the copier makes copying convenient and quicker.)
4. Have the note papers as well as source pages at the station. Students should use their library time to do their book research. They can do their Internet research as homework.
5. Demonstrate to the students how to make columns using Microsoft Word.

STATION 3: *ANIMAL FARM*—NEWSPAPER/TOPICS

1. The class will be divided into groups of 4–5 people.
2. Your group is to create a newspaper that reports the key events of the Russian Revolution and the eventual formation of the Communist country of USSR.
3. Each person in a group of 4 selects one set from 1–4. If there are five people, then use set 5.
4. Each person researches each of their topics, recording important information on note paper using the "reporter's questions": Who, What, Where, How, Why, So What?
5. Include your information in the form of newspaper content using at least 5 of the types listed below.

Types of Newspaper Content

Feature   Chart
Comic   Editorial
Advertisement   Map
Letters   Weather
Interview   Classified ad
Book review   Gossip column

6. Pictures should have captions, and stories and articles should have headlines.

Set 1

- Lenin
- Bolsheviks
- Siberia
- propaganda
- Pravda

Set 2

- Karl Marx
- workers/proletariats
- peasants
- oppression
- Communist Manifesto

Set 3

- Leon Trotsky
- White Russians

- Kremlin
- Secret Police: (Cheka/KGB)
- Politburo

Set 4

- Joseph Stalin
- Non-aggression pact with Hitler
- Collectivization of farms
- Moscow purge trials

Set 5

- Czar Nicholas II
- Alexander Kerensky
- Rasputin
- hammer and sickle flag
- "Red"

RESEARCH STEPS

1. Find and use at least one book and one Internet source on each topic.
2. Take notes keeping in mind the "reporter's questions."
3. Record bibliographic information for each source.
4. Use the search engines to locate sources on the Internet.

From *Collaborative Library Research Projects: Inquiry that Stimulates the Senses* by John D. Volkman. Westport, CT: Libraries Unlimited. Copyright © 2008.

GRADING

1. Newspaper   30 points   _____
   - Information on all 5 topics
   - Five different types of entries
   - Creativity

2. Bibliography   (10 points)
   - Sources all in one list alphabetically   1 point   _____
   - Book sources in proper form   3 points   _____
   - Internet sources in proper form   3 points   _____
   - Minimum of 3 types of sources   3 points   _____

3. Pictures   5 points   _____

4. Note papers (minimum of 10)   5 points   _____

5. Total   50 points   _____

STATION 4: *ANIMAL FARM*—BIOGRAPHY

Teacher Instructions

MATERIALS NEEDED

1. Same book and Internet sources used at station three.
2. Other sources of biographical information in your library should also be pointed out.
3. Note papers
4. Source pages with two books and two Internet sites, see Appendix 4.

STATION CONSTRUCTION

Set-up is the same as that for station three.

STATION 4: *ANIMAL FARM*—BIOGRAPHY

PERSON

The Russian Revolution produced a great array of political figures and leaders. In conjunction with researching your newspaper topics, you are going to write a short feature article that explores your person's power and his importance in Russian history. Your person is the first name listed in your Topic's set from Station 3: Set 1—Lenin, Set 2—Marx, Set 3—Trotsky, Set 4—Stalin, Set 5—Chose one of the persons listed: Nicholas II, Kerensky, or Rasputin.

Assignment

1. Write at least a two-page article addressing the following aspects of your person's life:
   - Personal background—family, education, upbringing, training
   - Description of his rise to power
   - His ideas and philosophy
   - His positions, title
   - How he used his power
   - Contributions to Russia
   - How he lost his power and/or died
   - Your evaluation of his role in the Russian Revolution and opinion of him as a leader

2. Include a page of pictures of your person and events related to him.
3. Include a Bibliography/Works Cited listing your sources in correct format.

RESEARCH STEPS

1. Find and use at least one book and one Internet source on your topic. Minimum of:
   - Six notes from book
   - Six notes from Internet source

2. Record bibliographic information for each source.
3. Use the search engines for Internet sources.

Suggested Resources

1. Biography or Russian history book
2. Biography reference books
3. Article from *Wilson Biographies* online or http://biography.com
4. Article from other Internet source

From *Collaborative Library Research Projects: Inquiry that Stimulates the Senses* by John D. Volkman. Westport, CT: Libraries Unlimited. Copyright © 2008.

Grading:

1. Written report (final copy)   15 points   _____
2. Bibliography   (5 points)
   - Sources all in one list alphabetically   1 point   _____
   - Book sources in proper form   2 points   _____
   - Internet sources in proper form   2 points   _____
3. Pictures   5 points   _____
4. Note papers (minimum of 12)   5 points   _____
5. Total   30 points   _____

CHAPTER 6

Shakespeare Stations

As the author of much of the literature that is studied by students, William Shakespeare makes a perfect subject for a station lesson. There are many ways that stations could be structured using websites, books, and media. The four stations shown here were developed for freshmen students reading *Romeo and Juliet* and are structured at a basic background level. The stations work equally well in preparing to read any of Shakespeare's plays. Books or websites that deal with the specific play being read could also be set up as stations for more sophisticated or non-freshmen students.

The first station is a video station, where students watch a video on Shakespeare's life. The one recommended here is the A&E Biography video, *William Shakespeare: A Life of Drama.* There are many others that libraries might choose to use that would work equally well.

Stations two and four both involve doing research on the students' topics. At station two, the students use the book resources and at station four, they use the online resources. The stations are set up so that the students do one research station each day along with one of the other stations. That way they are provided a change of pace during each period. To help keep the students on task and to be able to check that they are taking notes correctly and citing their sources properly, it is suggested that they finish a minimum number of notes each day in the library. These notes can be checked as the minimum is completed or at the end of the period and students given the points indicated on the cover page.

Station three is a favorite station because it exposes students to some of the many allusions, quotations, and sayings that have come into our everyday lexicon because of William Shakespeare's introducing us to them. Shakespeare is owed a great debt of gratitude for supplying so much of the idiom of the English language; it is a joy to share some of it with today's students.

Name _____

Teacher _____

Date _____ Period _____

Shakespeare Notebook

Cover Sheet

Your Points	Possible Points			
_____	20	**Station 1:**	**Video: "William Shakespeare: A Life of Drama"**	

    ◆ **Note 12 facts about Shakespeare.**

    ◆ **Type up a list of the 12 facts using complete sentences for each fact.**

    ◆ **Write out one short answer question about Shakespeare; include the answer to it.**

_____ 7   **Station 2:**   **Book Research**

    ◆ **Do research on your topic using books.**

    ◆ **Take notes and record sources.**

    ◆ **Finish 6 notes and source entry at end of period.**

_____ 25   **Station 3:**   **Computer Assignment**

    ◆ **Go to websites; look up allusions and quotations.**

    ◆ **Write out findings.**

_____ 7   **Station 4**   **Internet Research**

    ◆ **Do research on topic on Internet.**

    ◆ **Take notes and record sources.**

    ◆ **Finish 6 notes and source entry at end of period.**

_____ 41   **Research**   **Results from Stations 2 and 4**

    ◆ **Write 2 page essay (30 points).**

_____   ◆ **Bibliography in proper form (5 points).**

_____   ◆ **Additional Notes (6 points).**

_____

_____ 100   **Total Points**

_____   **Your Grade**

STATION 1: SHAKESPEARE—VIDEO

Teacher Instructions

MATERIALS NEEDED

William Shakespeare: A Life of Drama. A&E, 2004. $24.95. 50 minutes.

STATION CONSTRUCTION

1. Watch the video.
2. Edit and select the best 25–30 minutes so that you have a segment that will fit into the station time schedule.

STATION 1: SHAKESPEARE—VIDEO

In order to learn more about the life of William Shakespeare, you are going to watch the video, *William Shakespeare: A Life of Drama.* As you watch the video, note at least 12 facts about Shakespeare. You will then write out these facts in complete sentences and print a list of them using a word processing program. From the information you learned about Shakespeare, write out one short answer question that could be used on a quiz. Be sure to include the answer.

-
-
-
-
-
-
-
-
-
-
-
-

STATION 2: SHAKESPEARE: TOPICS—BOOK RESEARCH

Teacher Instructions

MATERIALS NEEDED

1.   Books with information on Elizabeth I, Elizabethan England, and William Shakespeare
2.   Note papers
3.   Shakespeare source page for books and internet sources (Note that the Shakespeare source page uses specific bibliographic examples for Shakespeare sources to help in teaching bibliographic formatting to beginning researchers.)

STATION CONSTRUCTION

1.   Put the books that have been pulled from the shelves on a book cart next to where the station is located. (Hint: Locating the station near the copier makes copying convenient and quicker.)
2.   Have the note papers as well as additional source pages at the station.

STATION 4: SHAKESPEARE: TOPICS—INTERNET RESEARCH

Teacher Instructions

MATERIALS NEEDED

1. Websites with information about Elizabethan England
2. Note papers
3. Source pages

STATION CONSTRUCTION

In the interest of saving search time and quickly getting students to useful sites, a list of suggested websites can be put on the library website. Some good Elizabethan websites are listed below by general topic and can easily be copied and posted on your website.

ELIZABETHAN ENGLAND WEBSITES

Life in Elizabethan England: A Compendium of Common Knowledge: http://elizabethan. org/compendium/home.html

Elizabethan England: Definitions of Elizabethan Terms & Everyday Life: http://www. springfield.k12.il.us/schools/springfield/eliz/elizabethanengland.html http://www. bardweb.net/england.html http://falcon.jmu.edu/~ramseyil/england.htm

Elizabeth I: http://www.elizabethi.org/us/

Crime and Punishment in Elizabethan England: http://www.eyewitnesstohistory.com/ punishment.htm http://ise.uvic.ca/Library/SLT/history/crimeandthelawsubj.html

Peasants and the Poor: http://www.saintives.com/essays/peasantlife.htm http://www. historylearningsite.co.uk/poor_in_elizabethan_england.htm

STATIONS 2 AND 4: SHAKESPEARE—TOPICS

ASSIGNMENT

In order to better understand the writings of William Shakespeare, it is helpful to know the background of his life and times. Each of you will have one of the topics below. You are to find information about your topic from at least one book and one Internet source. Take notes on the topic. You must have a minimum of six notes with proper citation of their source done at the end of each period in the library. Using your notes, you will then write a two-page essay describing your topic and why it is useful in understanding Shakespeare's plays.

TOPICS

1. Queen Elizabeth I
2. Globe Theatre
3. Medicine
4. Black Death
5. Peasant Life
6. City Life
7. Religion (Reformation)
8. Astrology
9. London—City Life
10. Music
11. Royalty/Monarchy
12. Women
13. Marriage
14. Children
15. James Burbage
16. Christopher Marlowe
17. Sports
18. Food and Drink
19. Clothing/Styles
20. Dentistry
21. War/Battles of the time in England
22. Acting Groups: Lord Chamberlain Players, The Queens Men
23. Education
24. Laws/Justice System
25. Transportation
26. Jobs
27. Anne Hathaway
28. Printing Industry
29. Crime
30. Criminal punishments

STATION 2—BOOK RESEARCH

1. Find and use books (at least one) on your topic.
2. Take notes on note paper.
3. Minimum of six notes.
4. Record bibliographic information for each book.
5. Be sure source number is on each note.

STATION 4—INTERNET RESEARCH

Use the library website or search engines to find websites that have information on Elizabethan England.

Take notes on note paper.

Minimum of six notes.

Record bibliographic information for each website.

Be sure source number is on each note.

From *Collaborative Library Research Projects: Inquiry that Stimulates the Senses* by John D. Volkman. Westport, CT: Libraries Unlimited. Copyright © 2008.

GRADING

1. Additional book notes, sources cited   3 points   _____
2. Additional Internet notes, sources cited   3 points   _____
3. Two Page Essay   30 points   _____
4. Note Cards/ Bibliography   (5 points)
    - Sources all in one list alphabetically   1 point   _____
    - Book sources in proper form   2 points   _____
    - Internet sources in proper form   2 points   _____
5. Total   41 points   _____

SOURCE PAGE

BOOK

1. _____ . _____
   AUTHOR (OR EDITOR)   TITLE of BOOK

   _____ . _____ :
                                                PLACE

   _____ , _____ . PAGES USED: _____ .
   PUBLISHER   YEAR PUBLISHED

Call Number

_____
_____
_____

BOOK

2. _____ . _____
   AUTHOR (OR EDITOR)   TITLE of BOOK

   _____ . _____ :
                                                PLACE

   _____ , _____ . PAGES USED: _____ .
   PUBLISHER   YEAR PUBLISHED

Call Number

_____
_____
_____

WEBSITE

3. _____ . _____ .
   AUTHOR (IF GIVEN)   NAME OF WEBPAGE OR ARTICLE

   _____ . _____
   DATE OF POSTING/REVISION   NAME OF ORGANIZATION AFFILIATED WITH SITE

   _____ . _____ .
   DATE YOU READ IT   ELECTRONIC ADDRESS (URL)

WEBSITE

4. _____ . _____ .
   AUTHOR (IF GIVEN)   NAME OF WEBPAGE OR ARTICLE

   _____ . _____
   DATE OF POSTING/REVISION   NAME OF ORGANIZATION AFFILIATED WITH SITE

   _____ . _____ .
   DATE YOU READ IT   ELECTRONIC ADDRESS (URL)

BIBLIOGRAPHIC EXAMPLES:

#1 – Smith, Ernest. *Elizabeth I*. Chicago: Harcourt, 2003.

#2 – Levy, Patricia. *English History*. New York: Marshall Cavendish, 2001.

#3 – Railton, Mark. *Weddings*. 2004. *Life in Elizabethan Times*. Feb. 3, 2006
        http://renaissance.dm.net/compendium/9.html.

#4 – "Crime and Punishment in Elizabethan England," EyeWitness to History, 2001. Feb. 24,
        2005. http://www.eyewitnesstohistory.com/punishment.htm.

STATION 3: SHAKESPEARE—COMPUTER ASSIGNMENT

Teacher Instructions

MATERIALS NEEDED

Reference books that contain Shakespeare quotations. There are many of these; here are three of the most familiar:

The Columbia Dictionary of Quotations from Shakespeare
Bartlett's Familiar Quotations
Shakespeare Quotations

STATION CONSTRUCTION

Make links on the library's website for:

http://www.cummingsstudyguides.net/xEveryday.html#Everyday%20Expressions
http://www.cummingsstudyguides.net/xQuotations.html#Quotations
http://www.allshakespeare.com/quotes/

Put the Shakespeare quotation books at the station.

STATION 3: SHAKESPEARE—COMPUTER ASSIGNMENT

ALLUSIONS AND QUOTATIONS FROM SHAKESPEARE

Allusion: A brief implied or indirect reference in literature to a person, event, or thing or to a part of another text. Most allusions are based on the assumption that there is a body of knowledge that is shared by the author and the reader and that therefore the reader will understand the author's reference. An allusion may be drawn from history, geography, literature, or religion.

- "The worst thing about missing an allusion is the fact that you didn't even know you missed it."
- Example: "That was a Hail-Mary pass." It is a desperate pass thrown at the end of a football game. If the listener didn't know that "Hail-Mary" refers to the Catholic practice of reciting the "Hail-Mary" prayer as an act of hope and request, he would not understand its usage.
- Shakespeare's writings contain more phrases that are in common usage than any other author's writings.
- There is the joke about the woman who read some Shakespeare plays and was asked how she liked them. She said they were good, but they contained "too many clichés." If you don't immediately understand this joke, then doing this station will aid that understanding.

Pick out three of the "Everyday Expressions" from the site below. Write each one down and briefly explain the allusion or what you think it means. http://sites.microlink. net/zekscrab/Expressions.html#Expressions

Expression #1:
Expression #2:
Expression #3:

Quotation: Repeating something someone spoke or wrote usually with credit acknowledgment. The works of Shakespeare are second only to the Bible in the frequency of passages being quoted.

Find two Shakespeare quotations, one from a quotation book and one from a website listed below:

http://sites.micro-link.net/zekscrab/quotations.html#Quotations
http://home.att.net/~quotations/shakespeare.html

For each quotation: write it down, cite what play it is taken from, what source you used, and then rewrite it in your own words showing what you think it means. If there are words you do not know the meaning of, look them up in a dictionary and mention what the definition is.

Quote #1:

Play:
Source:

From *Collaborative Library Research Projects: Inquiry that Stimulates the Senses* by John D. Volkman. Westport, CT: Libraries Unlimited. Copyright © 2008.

Rewrite:
Definitions:

Quote #2:

Play:
Source:
Rewrite:
Definitions:

CHAPTER 7

How to Develop and Implement Collaborative Research Units

Library assignments come in many shapes and sizes. The station units are large and multi-shaped and take much preparation time. The assignments in the succeeding chapters are more straightforward and less complicated. They do progress from assignments that have simpler end-products to those that have more sophisticated and creative end-products.

Each assignment begins with an explanation of the assignment along with general instructions for the librarian and teacher. A list of materials to prepare for the assignment is given, followed by how to construct the unit. Most of the assignments include some suggested book and Internet sources. These lists are only suggestions and are meant to give ideas on the types of resources to include. Many additional sources can be found on vendor web pages such as Amazon and Follett as well as in each library's own catalog.

The assignment sheet for the students follows the "Teacher Instructions." Each assignment includes some basic elements that are important in conveying to the students exactly what the expectations of them are. The elements that should be included are listed below:

1. Background and short description of why the subject is being researched
2. General description of the assignment
3. List of topics
4. List of suggested aspects of the topic to research and write about
5. Specific description of the end-product and what needs to be included in it
6. List of research steps, which can be divided into specific days in the library
7. List of suggested sources and/or ways to find the sources
8. Grading scale that specifies how many points each part of the assignment is worth

Each assignment includes the use of note papers and source pages. (Detailed information on source pages and note papers is found in Chapter 1.) Make the needed number of copies of the suggested source page for that assignment as well as plenty of note papers. With freshmen or classes that have not done research in your library, it is important to instruct them in proper note-taking and show them how to record their sources using the source pages. The source pages are designed so that the needed elements of the citation can simply be recorded on the source page in the order listed. On each note taken from a particular source, the student will simply put the number of the source as shown on the source page.

For shorter assignments, the source page used includes multiple types of resources. For assignments that require a lot of resources, the student can use source pages that include five of that type of resource. Point out to the students that the blanks for each source list the information needed for the bibliography in exactly the order required. The proper punctuation is also supplied on the source pages, so that the students can just transfer the information from the source page to their final bibliography.

The Internet has given students a wealth of information available at the click of a mouse. However, finding information, reading information, mentally processing information, citing the sources of information, and taking notes on information are all skills that students need to cultivate and improve. Whether information is found in a print source or on the Internet, the student still needs to follow those steps in order to learn and properly use it.

In order to encourage the use of these skills, the assignments all require multiple types of resources and always include the use of books. The basic information-processing skills are best taught and refined when using books. For many topics, useful information can be found in books in a quicker, more straightforward manner than on the Internet. Therefore, the assignments encourage students to use books first. In this way teachers can better control the use of the students' time in finding and citing sources and in taking the first set of notes. A key point to stress is that regardless of where the information is found, the student still needs to do something with it. And that something is read it, cite it, think about it, and take notes on it. Teachers should check that students are following those steps with the books they use before they are allowed to proceed to the Internet.

There are a couple of good research-teaching techniques that can be used in the library. As students are beginning their research, have each student show their first citation and first note to the teacher or librarian so that they can be checked that they are being done correctly. Putting a colorful sticker on each source page is a surprisingly effective motivator in getting students to work and do things quickly and properly. When students finish the minimum number of notes for that period, they can then get a sticker on their note paper as well as credit for their daily points.

Once students learn something about a topic using books, they can do more informed research on the Internet and hopefully be more discerning in selecting a site to use. Since searching the Internet can be a big time-waster if students just click around aimlessly instead of getting down to actually reading information on a site, it is imperative to keep them on task. Again, giving the students stickers and points are valuable in motivating students to have something written down as proof that they are actually working.

In conclusion, two of the goals of learning should be to make it a lifetime experience and to make it a fun and interesting proposition. These underlying goals are meant to be a part of all of these assignments and are goals that should be kept in mind as new units are developed.

CHAPTER 8

Drugs, Alcohol, and Smoking Research

Teacher Instructions

Doing a research project on drugs, alcohol, and smoking is a very common assignment and one for which materials are readily available in school libraries. Therefore, this assignment is set up to present a basic model for developing research projects. It has students consulting reference books, other nonfiction books, periodicals, and Internet sources. The students take notes from their sources, properly cite these sources, and write an essay.

There are numerous topics available on these subjects as well as multiple book and Internet sources. As such, it is a perfect assignment for teaching students how to access books using the library catalog. It is also an opportunity to teach the students how to find articles using periodical databases and search engines.

MATERIALS NEEDED

1. Reference books on drugs, alcohol, and smoking
2. Nonfiction books on drugs, alcohol, and smoking
3. Periodical databases

4.   Websites on drugs, alcohol, and smoking found using search engines.
5.   Note papers
6.   Source pages

UNIT CONSTRUCTION

1.   Source pages with two books, one periodical, and two Internet sites, see Appendix 5.
2.   Note papers

Drugs, Alcohol, and Smoking Research

ASSIGNMENT

The use of illegal drugs, alcohol, and tobacco by teenagers is a major problem in our society.

1. Choose alcohol, smoking, or a specific illegal drug.
2. Research your topic in four different sources.
3. Write a 500-word essay on the effect of your topic on teenagers in the United States.
4. Include a Bibliography/Works Cited listing your sources in correct format.

RESEARCH STEPS

1. Find and use at least one reference book. Take a minimum of 4 notes.
2. Find and use at least one nonfiction book. Take a minimum of 4 notes.
3. Find and use at least one periodical article. Take a minimum of 4 notes.
4. Find and use at least one website article. Take a minimum of 4 notes.
5. Record bibliographic information for each source on your source page.

SOURCES

Books

Use the library catalog to look up your topic. Look up the specific topic as well as the broader subject of Drugs, Alcohol, or Smoking.

Periodicals

Use the library's periodical database to find a magazine or newspaper article on your topic.

Websites

Use search engines such as Google, Yahoo, Ask.com, Dogpile.

Hint: Use the word "teenagers" along with drugs, alcohol, smoking, or specific name of drug, such as cocaine.

Grading

1.	Essay	74 points	_____
2.	Four different sources; minimum of 16 note papers	16 points	_____
3.	Bibliography	(10 points)	
	• Sources all in one list alphabetically	2 points	_____
	• Book sources in proper form	4 points	_____
	• Internet sources in proper form	4 points	_____
4.	Total	100 points	_____

CHAPTER 9

Evil Characters in History Research Paper

Teacher Instructions

Students, indeed, most people, are intrigued by the evil that is done in the world. There-fore, the natural fascination with evil is used as a hook in this lesson to get the students interested in the topic and in doing the research. The list of evil characters is endless, but the two websites listed below give a lot of good (bad?) choices. (Adolf Hitler is intention-ally left off the list because he is very familiar to all, and one of the goals of the unit is for the students to learn about new characters.)

Just as the list of evil characters is endless, so too is the list of resources. There are biographical reference books highlighting famous people in general and biographical reference books highlighting specific types of persons, by profession, nationality, or era. There are history reference books that include biographical information and there are full individual biographies. There are websites devoted to individuals and websites that include information on people within a larger framework.

Students need to learn to use these many types of resources; researching "evil char-acters" provides them that opportunity. In the process they can experience the fun of finding information and learning about fascinating characters. The "Evil Characters" unit is one that can be used for other subjects. The main aspects of a basic research paper are included in this unit and can serve as a prototype for other biography research papers. Instead of "evil characters" a teacher might assign a research paper on famous scientists, mathematicians, or artists. The research process is the same as it is for most library units: use the books on the first day and the Internet on the second day.

MATERIALS NEEDED

1. Source list showing the best sources for the information
2. Note papers
3. Source pages with two books and two Internet sites, see Appendix 4.

UNIT CONSTRUCTION

Choose which evil people to use for your choices.
A couple of good websites with suggested evil people are:

http://www.moreorless.au.com/
http://sprott.physics.wisc.edu/pickover/good.html

It is helpful to the students that the librarian do some "pre-research" and choose the people who can be found in the books in your library. The bibliography for the reference books is simply a starting point for students and is not all inclusive. Call numbers can be included on the resource list. Alternatively, the librarian can point out where the books are in the reference section or have the students look them up in the library catalog.

INSTRUCTIONS TO GIVE TO THE STUDENTS

1. Hand out the source lists and explain how to find the reference books in your library.
2. Remind students how to find books using your library's catalog.
3. Give everyone the yellow source page with two books and two Internet sources and a copy of the note paper.
4. Have additional note papers and source pages available.

EVIL CHARACTERS IN HISTORY

YOUR EVIL CHARACTER

History is replete with men and women who were bloodthirsty characters, evil to the core, and responsible for the death and torture of millions of innocent people. Your biographical research paper will focus on one of these evil people. You will choose your character from the list provided. You will write a five-page informative research paper that examines the life of your chosen malefactor. You must use at least two books and two Internet sources.

FORMAT

Your paper should follow this outline format:

1. Title Page
2. Table of Contents
3. Introduction
4. Personal Background
5. Rise to Power
6. Characteristics of His/Her Rule, Reign, or Influence
7. Downfall, Loss of Power, or Death
8. Conclusion
9. Bibliography/Works Cited Page
10. Appendix 1 (Map)
11. Appendix 2 (Timeline)

GRADING

1.	Outline	20 points	_____
2.	Draft	20 points	_____
3.	Title page	5 points	_____
4.	Table of Contents	5 points	_____
5.	Timeline (appendix 1)	5 points	_____
6.	Map (appendix 2)	5 points	_____
7.	Introduction	10 points	_____
8.	Three (3) content pages	50 points	_____
9.	Conclusion	10 points	_____
10.	Note papers (minimum of 20)	20 points	_____
11.	Organization	20 points	_____
12.	Grammar, spelling, punctuation	20 points	_____
13.	Bibliography/Works Cited	(10 points)	
	• Sources all in one list alphabetically	2 points	_____
	• Book sources in proper form	4 points	_____
	• Internet sources in proper form	4 points	_____
14.	Total	200 points	_____

DAY 1—BOOKS

1. Start with the *Reference (R) Books.*

   - Encyclopedia of World Biography
   - Twentieth-Century World Leaders
   - Historic World Leaders
   - Great Events
   - Man, Myth, and Magic
   - People's Almanac

2. Use the library catalog to look up topics such as:

   - Country of your person
   - Holocaust
   - Crime
   - Inquisition
   - Dictators
   - Leaders

3. At the end of the first period in the library, you must have *at least six notes* done with their book source properly recorded. You will have points deducted from "note papers" above if you do not.

DAY 2—INTERNET SOURCES

1. Use Wilson Biographies or www.biography.com.
2. Use search engines to look for the evil individuals.
3. Some good websites:

   http://www.moreorless.au.com/
   http://sprott.physics.wisc.edu/pickover/good.html

5. At the end of the second period in the library, you must have *at least 12 notes* done including six with their Internet source properly recorded. You will have points deducted from "note papers" above if you do not.

CHOOSE ONE OF THESE EVIL CHARACTERS

1. Idi Amin
2. Torquemada
3. Josef Mengele
4. Pizarro
5. Ivan the Terrible
6. Rasputin
7. Pol Pot
8. Lucrezia Borgia
9. Mobuto Sese Seko
10. Adolf Eichmann
11. Mao Tse-Tung
12. Joseph Stalin
13. Genghis Khan
14. Ataturk
15. Saddam Hussein
16. Robespierre
17. Nicolae Ceausescu
18. Benito Mussolini
19. Kim Il Sung
20. Francisco Franco
21. Slobodan Milosevic
22. Fidel Castro
23. Augusto Pinochet
24. Francois and Jean-Claude Duvalier
25. King Leopold II
26. Rafael Trujillo

CHAPTER 10

Edgar Allan Poe Poster and Report

Teacher Instructions

As discussed in the last chapter, research done on people such as authors, scientists, or other historical figures is some of the most interesting and easiest to do. The poster project on Edgar Allan Poe is a prototype of biographical research done in groups with a presentation as an end product. English classes often do this unit before the students read some of Poe's writings. The poster project can be adapted for researching other people or in introducing other units.

MATERIALS NEEDED

1. Reference books with information on the Edgar Allan Poe.
2. Be sure to look in author reference books, general biography reference books, and literature reference books.
3. Individual biographies of Poe.
4. Websites on Poe that are preselected or found using search engines.
5. Note papers.
6. Source pages with two books and two Internet sites, see Appendix 4.

UNIT CONSTRUCTION

1. Put the books that have been pulled from the shelves on a book cart next to where the station is located. (Hint: Locating the station near the copier makes copying convenient and quicker.)
2. Alternatively, if time and class size make it feasible, students can find books using your library's catalog.
3. Give everyone the yellow source page with two books and two Internet sources and a copy of the notepaper.

EDGAR ALLAN POE

ASSIGNMENT

In order to better understand Edgar Allan Poe and his writings, we will be doing research in the library. The class will be divided into groups (2–3 per group), which will each make a poster on one of the topics and present it to the class.

1. Poster explaining aspects of Edgar Allan Poe's life and work
2. Short presentation of the poster to the class (3–5 minutes)

TOPICS

1. Childhood, Upbringing
2. Education, Military
3. Alcohol, Gambling, Drugs
4. Wife and Family Life
5. Places He Lived
6. His Poetry
7. His Horror/Mystery Stories
8. Literary Critic and Magazine Writings
9. Last Two Years of Life, Death

POSTER BOARD CRITERIA

1. Poster Board—28" × 22"
2. Photos, drawings, graphs, or charts of people, events, places
3. Appropriate typed captions in your own words for each picture
4. Short typewritten word-processed information describing topic
5. Names of students in your group in the lower right hand corner of the front side
6. On back side write two questions that your fellow students should be able to answer after viewing your board

RESEARCH STEPS

1. Find and use at least one book and one Internet source on your topic. Minimum of:

   • Six notes from book
   • Six notes from Internet source

2. Record bibliographic information for each source.
3. Use the library website or search engines for Internet sources.

From *Collaborative Library Research Projects: Inquiry that Stimulates the Senses* by John D. Volkman. Westport, CT: Libraries Unlimited. Copyright © 2008.

GRADING

1. **Poster** (40 points)
   - The name of the author/topic prominently displayed — 5 points _____
   - Two quotations by or about Poe — 5 points _____
   - Timeline: birth, death and five major events on your topic — 5 points _____
   - Five interesting facts about your topic — 15 points _____
   - Four pictures or graphics related to the author and your topic — 5 points _____
   - Two questions about your topic — 5 points _____
2. Oral Presentation — 40 points _____
3. Minimum of 12 note papers — 12 points _____
4. **Bibliography** (8 points)
   - Sources all in one list alphabetically — 2 points _____
   - Book sources in proper form — 3 points _____
   - Internet sources in proper form — 3 points _____
6. Total — 100 points _____

Poster Board Instructions

1. Size: 28" × 22"

2. Title:
Place a title at the top using the name of your topic in large letters.

3. Pictures:
Use photos or drawings of people, stories, places in Poe's life

4. Captions:
Type appropriate captions for each picture

5. Written information:
Include important facts, quotations in brief, typed form

EDGAR ALLAN POE

Poe was a melancohly man.

Written information could go here:_____
_____
_____

Quotations: "Quoth the raven, 'Nevermore.'"

More written information could go here:_____
_____
_____
_____

Written information could go here:_____
_____
_____

The Raven

Born	*Raven* pub.	Died
1809	1845	1849

Names of students in your group

6. Quotations:
From Poe or about Poe.

7. Questions:
On bottom left of back side write 2 questions that can be answered by viewing your board.

8. Timeline or chart:
Create your own timeline showing the major events in Poe's life.

9. Names:
Place your names in the lower right-hand corner.

CHAPTER 11

Children of the River Poster and Report

Teacher Instructions

Students in English/literature classes across the country read novels as part of the basic curriculum. One way to motivate teachers to use the library as a part of their students' study of a book is to present them with a simple project that will not take a lot of class time, but will still impart to the students valuable information and invaluable research skills. A poster project such as this one on the *Children of the River* (Linda Crew, New York: Delacorte, 1989) is a great way for students to learn background on the book and to pique their interest in it.

Similar to the Edgar Allan Poe poster project, this poster project on *Children of the River* is a prototype for setting up a research project in conjunction with a novel that a class is reading. Select the topics to be researched by looking at the setting of the book and other aspects of the environment in which the characters live. Also, consider the themes that are explored. Even the personality traits of the characters can provide topics. Then check to be sure that there is adequate information in the books and websites to adequately address each topic.

MATERIALS NEEDED

1. Books with information on Cambodia and the other topics on the list.
2. Websites on Cambodia:
    http://www.infoplease.com/ipa/A0107378.html
    http://www.tourismcambodia.com/
3. There are three websites that are especially good for country research:
    Background Notes: http://www.state.gov/r/pa/ei/bgn/
    CIA Factbook: https://www.cia.gov/library/publications/the-world-factbook/index.
        html
    Visual Geography: http://www.vgsbooks.com/
4. Note papers
5. Source pages with two books and two Internet sites, see Appendix 4.

UNIT CONSTRUCTION

1. Put the books that have been pulled from the shelves on a book cart next to where the station is located. (Hint: Locating the station near the copier makes copying convenient and quicker.)
2. Alternatively, if time and class size make it feasible, students can find books using your library's catalog.
3. Put the suggested links on the library website.
4. Give everyone the yellow source page with 2 books and 2 Internet sources and a copy of the note paper.

CHILDREN OF THE RIVER

ASSIGNMENT

In order to better understand the book, *Children of the River* by Linda Crew, we will be learning about a number of topics related to Cambodia and some of the themes in the book. You will each make a poster and present it to the class.

1. Poster explaining your topic
2. Short presentation of the poster to the class (2–3 minutes)
3. Minimum of two books and two Internet sources

TOPICS

1. Interracial Dating
2. Southeast Asians' Immigration to United States
3. King Sihanouk
4. Khmer Rouge
5. Killing Fields
6. Angkor Wat
7. Pol Pot

Cambodia:

1. Daily Life
2. Religions
3. Weddings/Dating Customs
4. Land/Climate
5. Food
6. Cities
7. Government
8. Pre-1900 History
9. Post-1900 History
10. Clothing
11. Economy
12. Farming and Fishing
13. Languages
14. Education
15. Customs/Festivals
16. Arts/Entertainment

POSTER BOARD CRITERIA

1. Size: 28" × 22"
2. Contents:

    • Photos, drawings, graphs, or charts of people, events, places
    • Appropriate typed captions in your own words for each picture
    • Two word-processed paragraphs highlighting your topic (five sentences per paragraph)

3. On back side write two questions that your fellow students should be able to answer after viewing your board.

GRADING

1.	Poster	45 points	_____
2.	Oral Report	25 points	_____
3.	Note papers (minimum of 20)	20 points	_____
4.	Bibliography/Works Cited	(10 points)	
	• Sources all in one list alphabetically	2 points	_____
	• Book sources in proper form	4 points	_____
	• Internet sources in proper form	4 points	_____
5.	Total	100 points	

RESEARCH STEPS/SOURCES

Day 1	Day 2
Books	**Internet**
Books on Cambodia	Websites on Cambodia: http://www.info please.com/ipa/A0107378.html http://www. tourismcambodia.com/
Country Encyclopedias	There are three websites that are especially good for country research:
Reference books on world leaders	Background Notes: http://www.state.gov/r/ pa/ei/bgn/
World cultures books	CIA Factbook: https://www.cia.gov/library/ publications/the-world-factbook/index.html
Reference books on sociology	Visual Geography: http://www.vgsbooks. com/
Books on interracial dating	Use search engines, Wilson Biographies.
At the end of the first period in the library, you must have at least six notes done with their book sources properly recorded. You will have points deducted from "note papers" above if you do not.	At the end of the second period in the library, you must have at least 12 notes done including six with their Internet sources properly recorded. You will have points deducted from "note papers" above if you do not.

Poster Board Instructions

1. Size: 28" × 22"

2. Title:
Place a title at the top using the name of your topic in large letters.

3. Pictures:
Use photos or drawings of people, events, places.

4. Captions:
Type appropriate captions for each picture.

5. Other pictures with captions

CAMBODIAN LIFE

Cambodian fisherman displays what he uses to fish with.

Written information could go here:_____
_____
_____

6. Written information:
Paragraph including important facts in brief, typed form

The flag of Cambodia has three-towered temple representing Angor Wat.

7. Questions:
On bottom left of back side write 2 questions that can be answered by viewing your board.

More written information could go here:_____
_____
_____
_____

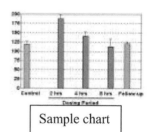

Sample chart

Kara June, per. 5

8. Timeline or chart:
Show events or statistics in graphical form.

9. Your name: Bottom right

CHAPTER 12

Decades: *Of Mice and Men, The Human Comedy,* and "We Didn't Start the Fire"

Whether American history is studied directly in history classes or indirectly in English classes reading various novels, it is often useful to study the history as it is broken down into decades. The research assignments that follow give examples of the ways that librarians can develop units with their teachers that will allow the teachers to involve their students in the process of learning American history. The assignments are similar to the previous poster projects but also include topics and resources that are specific to their subjects. They can be used with the specific novels indicated or easily adapted to other novels whose historic settings are important to the understanding of the books.

During the last few years, many publishers have met the need for history reference books that are divided by decades. There are also many sets that highlight specific categories of people such as athletes, authors, or musicians. In teaching students the research process, it is important for them to learn about the many specialized reference books that are available in addition to the basic general subject encyclopedias. Some of the most important of these books are listed in the units. Additionally, there are numerous websites dedicated to describing the decades and the people and events associated with them. Some of them are also included on the worksheets. Websites that deal with specific people and events can easily be located using a search engine.

The units on *Of Mice and Men, The Human Comedy,* and "We Didn't Start the Fire" all make use of reference books dedicated to the decades of U.S. history.

Here are some suggested reference sets on the decades in U.S. history:

America in the 20th Century. New York: Marshall Cavendish, 2003. 13 vols. $439.95. 0–7614–7364–5.

American Decades. Detroit: Thomson/Gale, 1995. 10 vols. $1095. 0–8103–5726–7.

Great Events from History: The 20th Century. Pasadena, Calif.: Salem Press, 2002. 8 vols. $499. 1–58765–061–4.

Pendergast, Sara, and Tom Pendergast. *Bowling, Beatniks, and Bell-Bottoms: Pop Culture of 20th-Century America.* Detroit, Mich.: UXL/Thomson/Gale, 2002. 5 vols. op. 0–7876–5676–3.

UXL American Decades. Detroit, Mich.: UXL/Thomson/Gale, 2003. 10 vols. $495. 0–7876–6454–5.

OF MICE AND MEN

Teacher Instructions

The decade of the Great Depression, 1930–1939, is the backdrop for *Of Mice and Men* (John Steinbeck, New York: Viking, 1937). To help the students better understand what life was like during that time, it is good to select topics that reflect all aspects of life. The list included covers many of these aspects and can easily be expanded to include many other related people and events.

MATERIALS NEEDED

1. Reference sets on the decades in American history
2. Reference sets on the Great Depression such as:
   Depression America. Danbury, Conn.: Grolier Educational, 2001. 6 vols. $319. 0–7172–5502–6.
3. Biography reference books that include the people selected
4. Some useful websites on the decades:
   http://kclibrary.nhmccd.edu/decades.html
   http://www.infoplease.com/yearby year.html
   http://history1900s.about.com/od/1930s/1930_1939.htm
   http://dir.yahoo.com/Arts/Humanities/History/U_S__History/By_Time_Period/20th_Century/1930s
   http://www.teacheroz.com/20thcent.htm#30s
5. Note papers
6. Source pages with two books and two Internet sites, see Appendix 4.

UNIT CONSTRUCTION

1. Make a source list that highlights some of the most useful sets and indicates the general call numbers of some categories of subjects. Students can certainly find some of the books using the library's catalog, but it can be very helpful to include some of the broader topics that they might search.
2. Put the suggested links on the library website.
3. Give everyone the yellow source page with two books and two Internet sources and a copy of the note paper.

OF MICE AND MEN

ASSIGNMENT

Imagine that you are able to step back in time—back to the decade of America's Great Depression, 1930–1939. Your time machine has transported you back to briefly investigate this decade. What would life be like for someone living then? What would people wear and where would they live? What would they do for entertainment: go to the movies, watch television, listen to the radio? What important events would be occurring and who are the newsmakers?

Your job is to investigate and report to the class what you found out about the specific person, event, or thing you investigated. When your investigation is completed, you will make an oral presentation (3–5 minutes) to the class. In the presentation, utilize posters, pictures, graphics, music, video, or objects to illustrate what you are presenting. You will also write a brief essay (2–3 pages) describing your subject. You must use a minimum of two books and two Internet sources.

TOPICS

1. Franklin D. Roosevelt
2. Stock Market Crash
3. Bank Failures
4. Hoovervilles
5. Unemployment
6. Babe Ruth
7. Bobby Jones
8. Hawley-Smoot Tariff
9. Empire State Building
10. Mount Rushmore
11. Hoover Dam
12. Lindbergh Kidnapping
13. Dust Bowl
14. Shirley Temple
15. Charlie Chaplin
16. Al Capone
17. Route 66
18. *Gone With the Wind* (book)
19. *Our Town* (play)
20. *War of the Worlds* (radio program)
21. New Deal
22. Joe Louis
23. National Industrial Recovery Act
24. Labor Unions
25. Amelia Earhart
26. Jesse Owens

GRADING

1.	Essay (2–3 page final copy)	30 points	_____
2.	First draft	10 points	_____
3.	Poster, graphics, music, video, objects	15 points	_____
4.	Oral Report	15 points	_____
5.	Note papers (minimum of 20)	20 points	_____
6.	Bibliography/Works Cited	(10 points)	
	• Sources all in one list alphabetically	2 points	_____
	• Book sources in proper form	4 points	_____
	• Internet sources in proper form	4 points	_____
7.	Total	100 points	_____

From *Collaborative Library Research Projects: Inquiry that Stimulates the Senses* by John D. Volkman. Westport, CT: Libraries Unlimited. Copyright © 2008.

RESEARCH STEPS/SOURCES

Day 1

At the end of the first period in the library, you must have at least eight notes from at least two sources with correct citation information recorded. You will have points deducted from "note papers" above if you do not.

Day 2

At the end of the second period in the library, you must have at least 16 notes from at least two sources with correct citation information recorded. You will have points deducted from "note papers" above if you do not.

Resources for the 1930s

1. *General Reference (R) sources to use*

Various books on the 1930s in World History such as:

- *Chronicle of the 20th Century* 1 vol.
- *Dictionary of American History* 10 vols.
- *Great Events from History,* 3 vols.
- *Great Events: The Twentieth Century,* v. 2, 1920–1959
- *History of the 20th Century*
- *365 Most Important Events of the 20th Century*

Various books on decades in United States history such as:

- *America in the Twentieth Century,* v. 4, 1930–1939
- *American Decades, 1930–1939*
- *American Heritage Encyclopedia of American History*
- *Bowling, Beatniks, and Bell-Bottoms: Pop Culture of 20th Century America,* v. 2, 1920s–1930s
- *Encyclopedia of World Biography,* 19 vols., plus supplements
- *This Fabulous Century, 1930s*
- *Fashions of a Decade*

2. *Specialized reference or regular books in Dewey Decimal categories such as the following*

796	Sports
791.43	Movies
809	Authors
364	Crime and Criminals
709	Art and Artists
780	Music and Musicians
629.222	Automobiles

3. ***Library Catalog***

   United States-History-1933–1945
   Depressions-1929-United States
   Motion Pictures
   Fashion-History
   Comic books, strips, etc.

4. ***Websites with which to start***

   http://kclibrary.nhmccd.edu/decades.html
   http://www.infoplease.com/yearbyyear.html
   http://melvil.chicousd.org/decsg.html
   http://dir.yahoo.com/Arts/Humanities/History/U_S__History/By_Time_Period/
   20th_Century/1930s/
   http://www.teacheroz.com/20thcent.htm#30s
   Search Engines

THE HUMAN COMEDY

Teacher Instructions

The *Human Comedy* (William Sarayon, New York: Harcourt, Brace and Company, 1943) is set during World War II, which was primarily the decade of the 1940s. The book deals with everyday people doing everyday things during an extraordinary period of American history. Therefore, the topics on the list deal with the common aspects of life. These generic topics allow the students wide latitude in choosing the emphasis of their research and presentation. Depending on the level of the students, the topics could also be chosen so as to be more specific, as they were in the *Of Mice and Men* lesson.

MATERIALS NEEDED

1.   Reference books on the decade of the 1940s
2.   Reference books on World War II
3.   Reference books on Fresno and California
4.   Some useful websites on decades:

   http://kclibrary.nhmccd.edu/decades.html
   http://www.infoplease.com/yearbyyear.html
   http://history1900s.about.com/od/1940s/1940_1949.htm
   http://dir.yahoo.com/Arts/Humanities/History/U_S__History/By_Time_Period/
      20th_Century/1940s/
   http://www.teacheroz.com/wwii.htm

5.   Note papers
6.   Source pages with two books and two Internet sites, see Appendix 4.

UNIT CONSTRUCTION

1.   Make a source list that highlights some of the most useful sets and indicates the general call numbers of some categories of subjects.
2.   Put the suggested links on the library website.
3.   Give everyone the yellow source page with two books and two Internet sources and a copy of the notepaper.

THE HUMAN COMEDY

ASSIGNMENT

William Saroyan's book, *The Human Comedy,* is set in Fresno, California during World War II. He described everyday people going about their lives in a nation united in fighting a war against a common enemy. What were Fresno and California like over 60 years ago? What would life be like for someone living in the United States during World War II? How did the war affect the people regarding the work they did, the homes they lived in, and the clothes they wore? With the war as an ever present reality, what would people do for entertainment?

In order to find answers to these questions, you will put together a 2–3 page report on a topic related to this era. In the report you will include the following elements:

1. Description of the topic as related to the 1940s
2. Examples of the topic
3. Explanation of how the topic was influenced by the ongoing war
4. Two excerpts or quotations from your research on the topic
5. Graphics: drawings, magazines pictures, photocopies, or computer pictures that tie in to your topic
6. Personal response to what you discovered in the form of comments, interpretations, and evaluations

You must use a minimum of two books and two Internet sources.

TOPICS

1. Clothing
2. Cooking
3. Technology
4. Jobs
5. Hairstyles
6. Government
7. Homes
8. Toys
9. News
10. Popular Books
11. Jingles
12. Movies
13. Sports
14. Transportation
15. Food and Drink
16. Music
17. Television
18. Radio
19. Medicine
20. Education
21. Cultures
22. Religion
23. Economy
24. Employment
25. Advertisements
26. Farming/Agriculture
27. Consumer Products

From *Collaborative Library Research Projects: Inquiry that Stimulates the Senses* by John D. Volkman. Westport, CT: Libraries Unlimited. Copyright © 2008.

GRADING

1. Essay (2–3 page final copy)   45 points   _____
2. First draft   10 points   _____
3. Graphics   15 points   _____
4. Note papers (minimum of 20)   20 points   _____
5. Bibliography/Works Cited   (10 points)
    - Sources all in one list alphabetically   2 points   _____
    - Book sources in proper form   4 points   _____
    - Internet sources in proper form   4 points   _____
6. Total   100 points   _____

RESEARCH STEPS/SOURCES

Day 1

At the end of the first period in the library, you must have at least eight notes from at least two sources with correct citation information recorded. You will have points deducted from "note papers" above if you do not.

Day 2

At the end of the second period in the library, you must have at least 16 notes from at least two sources with correct citation information recorded. You will have points deducted from "note papers" above if you do not.

Resources for the 1940s

1. *General Reference (R) sources to use*

Various books on 1940s in world history such as

- *Chronicle of the 20th Century,* 1 vol.
- *Dictionary of* American *History,* 10 vols.
- *Great Events: The Twentieth Century,* v. 3, 1940–1959
- *Great Events from History,* 3 vols.
- *History of the 20th Century*
- *365 Most Important Events of the 20th Century*

Various books on decades in United States history such as

- *America in the Twentieth Century,* v. 5, 1940–1949
- *American Decades, 1940–1949*
- *American Heritage Encyclopedia of American History*
- *As Pop Saw It (Fresno)*
- *Bowling, Beatniks, and Bell-Bottoms: Pop Culture of 20th Century America,* v. 3, 1940's–1950's

- *Fashions of a Decade*
- *Garden of the Sun* (History of Fresno County)
- *An Illustrated History of Fresno County*
- *This Fabulous Century, 1940s*
- World War II books

3. Library Catalog:

United States History, 1933–1945
World War II
Motion Pictures
Fashion-History
Comic books, strips, etc.

4. Websites with which to start:

http://kclibrary.nhmccd.edu/decades.html
http://www.infoplease.com/yearbyyear.html
http://history1900s.about.com/od/1940s/1940_1949.htm
http://dir.yahoo.com/Arts/Humanities/History/U_S__History/By_Time_Period/
    20th_Century/1940s/
http://www.teacheroz.com/wwii.htm

"WE DIDN'T START THE FIRE"

Teacher Instructions

In 1989 Billy Joel released "We Didn't Start the Fire," which reached number 1 on the *Billboard* record chart. The song's numerous historical references make it a natural hook for getting students interested in learning more about history. There are a number of websites that present the song in video format and explain the historical illusions. The interactive nature of these websites helps heighten student interest in the project. There are also many great reference books that cover the decades, the events of them, and the people involved in them. As the research takes place, be sure to observe the students browse these books, discover intriguing historical facts, and then excitedly share them with their group.

There are seven sets of subjects listed for each decade. If there are fewer than seven students in a group, then "Law, Business" can be combined with "Government, Politics" (and with "International Events, Wars," if needed) and "Health, Medicine" can be combined with "Science, Inventions, Technology."

MATERIALS NEEDED

1. Reference books on the decades, 1940–1989
   In addition to the sets covering the whole twentieth century, there are good sets on each decade, such as those listed below:
   The Fifties in America. Pasadena, Calif.: Salem Press, 2005. 3 vols. $364. 978–1–58765–202–8.
   The Seventies in America. Pasadena, Calif.: Salem Press, 2005. 3 vols. $364. 978–1-58765–228–8
   The Sixties in America. Pasadena, Calif.: Salem Press, 1999. 3 vols. $364. 978–0–89356–982–2.
2. Biography reference books
3. Websites on decades listed on the assignment sheet below
4. Bulleted note papers, see Appendix 6
5. Book source pages, see Appendix 1
6. Internet source pages, see Appendix 2

UNIT CONSTRUCTION

1. Put the suggested links on the library website.
2. Find the books on the library shelves that deal with the decades.
3. Make a stack of books for each of the decades, 1940–1989, and put them on separate tables.
4. Show the students the video on the website, http://www.ugoplayer.com/music/fire.html, which presents pictures of the events mentioned in the song as it plays.
5. Have each group of students sit at the table that has the books for their decade. Having the students sit this way facilitates their ability to browse the books and pick out the topics that they want to research for their decade. As students find topics of interest, they can then find additional books using the library's catalog. Give each student two of the "Bulleted Note Pages." On the first day, give each student one of the "Book Source Pages." On the second day, give each student one of the "Internet Source Pages."

DECADES

"We Didn't Start the Fire" by Billy Joel

ASSIGNMENT

"Billy Joel (reportedly) wrote this song because he overheard a child say that he felt sorry for 'older people' like Billy Joel because no 'history' happened in their lifetime, that NOW (or the time the song was written) was going to be the world's most historical time period. The comment got to Billy Joel so much that he sat down and wrote this to prove that his lifetime has been FULL of history." (EZHOMUZIC. *We Didn't Start the Fire*. November 28, 2006. *Information and Trivia*. http://contactezhomuzic.blogspot.com/2006/11/billy-joesl.html.)

Your assignment is to find out the truth of Billy Joel's thoughts by researching some of the history of each of the last five decades. You will be in a group of 4–7 people that will explore one decade and then make a presentation to the class explaining what you found. Each person in your group will have a general subject for which they will find five significant topics (events or persons) and then find information about each of them. The information you find will be presented on a poster board or PowerPoint presentation to the rest of the class.

RESEARCH STEPS

Day 1

Book

Books on decades in U.S. history: Each person in the group chooses one of the subjects listed below. For their subject area, each person will find five topics that they will research. They will then find five facts about each of them using the books and record them on their note papers. Record source number and page number on each note.

Day 2

Internet

http://www.school-for-champions.com/history/start_fire_facts.htm
http://www.teacheroz.com/fire.htm
http://www.ugoplayer.com/music/fire.html
http://en.wikipedia.org/wiki/We_Didn't_Start_the_Fire
http://kclibrary.nhmccd.edu/decades.html
http://www.infoplease.com/yearbyyear.html
http://melvil.chicousd.org/decsg.html

Using the websites above or other websites, each person will find five more facts about each of the topics that they researched using the books the first day. They will record them on the note papers along with the proper bibliographic information.

SUBJECTS

1. Government, Politics
2. Science, Inventions, Technology
3. Culture: Radio Shows, Television Shows, Movies, Books, Arts, Fashion, Fads
4. Sports: Teams, Athletes, Olympics
5. International Events, Wars
6. Law, Business
7. Health, Medicine

As you do your research, look for answers to these questions:

How would the event/person be described?
Why was this event/person important?
What was the background of this event/person?
How did this event/person influence or affect Americans?
How did this event/person change/improve America?

MY FIVE TOPICS

Presentation Requirements

Poster: 28" × 22" or PowerPoint presentation with 15–20 slides
Contents:

- Photos or drawings of pertinent people, events, places
- Appropriate word-processed captions in your own words for each picture
- Short, word-processed information describing topics
- Your names on the back of the poster or end of the PowerPoint presentation

GRADING

1.	Note papers (10 minimum)	30 points	_____
2.	Bibliography	(10 points)	
	• Sources all in one list alphabetically	2 points	_____
	• Book sources in proper form	4 points	_____
	• Internet sources in proper form	4 points	_____
3.	Poster or PowerPoint presentation	40 points	_____
4.	Oral presentation	20 points	_____
5.	Total	100 points	_____

CHAPTER 13

Constellations and the Zodiac Poster and Report

Teacher Instructions

Most students have at least a passing interest in stars and constellations as well as in mythology. Studying astronomy by way of researching the signs of the zodiac is a great way to tap into that natural curiosity. Most libraries have a number of books on constellations, the zodiac, and mythology, so this combination of subjects utilizes readily available library materials. Additionally, websites abound on these subjects. Because this assignment is designed for students who are just learning research on the Internet, annotations of the websites have been included on the assignment sheet.

MATERIALS NEEDED

1. Books with information on astronomy, constellations, zodiac, and mythology
2. Note papers
3. Source pages with encyclopedia, book, and two Internet sites, see Appendix 7

UNIT CONSTRUCTION

1. Put the books that have been pulled from the shelves on a book cart next to where the station is located. (Hint: Locating the station near the copier makes copying convenient and quicker.)
2. Alternatively, if time and class size make it feasible, students can find books using your library's catalog.
3. Put the suggested links on the library website.
4. Give everyone the source page with encyclopedia, book, and two Internet sites, and a copy of the note paper.

CONSTELLATIONS AND THE ZODIAC

ASSIGNMENT

To learn more about stars and constellations, we will be doing research in the library. The zodiac (from the ancient Greek word meaning circle of animals) is a band-shaped section of the sky that contains 12 special constellations. These constellations (also called signs) are also the names seen in horoscopes: Aries, Taurus, Gemini, Cancer, Leo, Virgo, Libra, Scorpio, Sagittarius, Capricorn, Aquarius, and Pisces.

Choose the sign for your birthday. (You can quickly find it in any newspaper or encyclopedia or on the Internet.) Then find the following information about the constellation:

1. Name and dates of the constellation: calendar dates when the constellation is visible in the sky.
2. Location of constellation: hemisphere, nearby constellations or "landmark" structures.
3. Description of the constellation: what it looks like; name of significant stars, galaxies, or structures; number of stars/structures in it.
4. Mythology or history: story or stories behind the constellation. Is it a myth or does it have historical ties to real people or both?

TO BE TURNED IN

1. Poster
2. Written report of information

RESEARCH STEPS

1. You will be using at least three sources: one encyclopedia, one book, one Internet website
2. Find and use at least one encyclopedia and one book about your constellation.
3. Take a minimum of two notes from the encyclopedia and four notes from the book.

BOOKS

Encyclopedias (Look under name of sign/constellation)
Look in the library catalog for books on these subjects: Astronomy, Stars, Mythology

INTERNET

Find and use at least one Internet source on your topic.
Record bibliographic information for each source you use.
Minimum of four notes from Internet sources such as those listed below:
Constellations and their Stars: http://www.astro.wisc.edu/~dolan/constellations/
Explains what constellations are, lists stars and constellations alphabetically. Includes interactive star chart and a brief explanation of the myths behind the names of many of the constellations.

From *Collaborative Library Research Projects: Inquiry that Stimulates the Senses* by John D. Volkman. Westport, CT: Libraries Unlimited. Copyright © 2008.

Astronomical Society (Peoria): http://www.astronomical.org/
Information about the constellations including star maps and data for each.
Hawaiian Astronomical Society: www.hawastsoc.org/deepsky/constellations.html
The constellations arranged alphabetically with myths, maps, and images.
Enchanted Learning: http://www.enchantedlearning.com/subjects/astronomy/stars/constellations.shtml
Descriptions and maps of the zodiac constellations.
Signs of the Zodiac: http://www.dacha.freeuk.com/zodiac/esoz-0.htm
Myths and legends of the zodiac signs.
Use search engines such as Google, looking for sites that end in .edu or .org.

GRADING

Poster

After finding the above information, you will make a poster (22" × 28") that is creative, informative, and must include the following (minimum requirements):

1.	Name of the sign prominently displayed	5 points	_____
2.	Dates of the sign	5 points	_____
3.	Astrological information	5 points	_____
4.	Drawing of the star pattern, other significant stars, galaxies, astrological structures	5 points	_____
5.	Mythological and historical information	10 points	_____
6.	Creativity and neatness	15 points	_____

Written Report

7.	Paragraph on each of these topics:		
8.	Introduction	5 points	_____
9.	Description of constellation, other significant stars, galaxies, astrological structures	10 points	_____
10.	Mythological or historical information	10 points	_____
11.	Astrological information	5 points	_____
12.	Conclusion	5 points	_____
13.	Note papers (minimum of 10)	10 points	_____
14.	Bibliography/Works Cited	(10 points)	
	• Sources all in one list alphabetically	2 points	_____
	• Book sources in proper form	4 points	_____
	• Internet sources in proper form	4 points	_____
15.	Total	100 points	_____

CHAPTER 14

Rocks and Minerals
Poster and Report

Teacher Instructions

Students in science classes have many different terms or concepts that they must learn. Most of these concepts are taught using science textbooks. In order to encourage science teachers to use the library for learning these concepts, librarians can develop lessons such as this one on "Rocks and Minerals" that incorporate library research into the learning process. Both teachers and students enjoy the opportunity to work outside the classroom and have a change of pace from the daily classroom routine.

Similar to the English poster projects, this poster project on "Rocks and Minerals" can be used as a format for setting up similar science projects. In determining what science units will work in the library, be sure to check that there is adequate information in the library books and on Internet websites.

MATERIALS NEEDED

1. Books with information on rocks and minerals
2. Websites on rocks and minerals:

http://www.galleries.com/default.htm

http://geology.about.com/od/nutshells/a/whatisgeology.htm

3. Note papers
4. Source pages with two books and two Internet sites, see Appendix 4.

UNIT CONSTRUCTION

1. Put the books that have been pulled from the shelves on a book cart next to where the station is located. (Hint: Locating the station near the copier makes copying convenient and quicker.)
2. Alternatively, if time and class size make it feasible, students can find books using your library's catalog.
3. Put the suggested links on the library website.
4. Give everyone the yellow source page with two books and two Internet sources and a copy of the note paper.

ROCKS AND MINERALS

ASSIGNMENT

1.   Pretend that you are a geologist who is classifying rocks and minerals.
2.   It is your job to research one of the rocks and minerals listed below:

- Alabaster
- Asbestos
- Azurite
- Basalt
- Bauxite
- Calcite
- Chalk
- Cinnabar
- Copper
- Coral
- Corundum
- Diamond
- Feldspar
- Flint
- Fluorite
- Gold
- Graphite

- Gypsum
- Hornblende
- Limestone
- Limonite
- Lodestone
- Marble
- Mica
- Obsidian
- Pumice
- Pyrite
- Quartz
- Salt
- Sandstone
- Shale
- Silicon
- Silver
- Slate

3.   Prepare a poster highlighting aspects of your rock or mineral such as those below:

- Hardness
- Shape
- Composition
- Size
- Uses
- Chemical composition

- Color
- Luster
- Cleavage
- Location in the World
- History

4.   Use your poster board to make an oral report to the class describing your mineral or rock (2–3 minutes).

RESEARCH STEPS

1.   Find and use at least one book about rocks and minerals that has information on your topic.
2.   Take a minimum of four notes from the book.
3.   Find and use at least one Internet source on your topic.
4.   Use a search engine or these two websites:

http://www.galleries.com/default.htm
http://geology.about.com/od/nutshells/a/whatisgeology.htm

From *Collaborative Library Research Projects: Inquiry that Stimulates the Senses* by John D. Volkman. Westport, CT: Libraries Unlimited. Copyright © 2008.

5. Record bibliographic information for each source you use.

6. Minimum of four notes from Internet source.

POSTER BOARD CRITERIA

1. Size: 28" × 22"

2. Contents:

   - Photos, drawings, maps of your topic
   - Appropriate word-processed captions in your own words for each graphic
   - Two word-processed paragraphs highlighting your topic (five sentences per paragraph)
   - Your name in the lower right hand corner of the front side
   - On back side write two questions that other students can answer after reading your poster

GRADING

1.	Poster	20 points	_____
2.	Oral Report	17 points	_____
3.	Note papers (minimum of 8)	8 points	_____
4.	Bibliography/Works Cited	(5 points)	
	• Sources all in one list alphabetically	1 point	_____
	• Book sources in proper form	2 points	_____
	• Internet sources in proper form	2 points	_____
5.	Total	50 points	_____

Rock/Mineral Poster Example

1. Size: 28" × 22"

GOLD

2. Title:
Place a title at the top using the name of your topic in large letters.

3. Pictures:
Use photos or drawings of your topic.

4. Captions:
Type appropriate captions for each picture.

5. Written information:
Include important facts in a paragraph.

| 79 |
| AU |
| Gold |
| 196.96655 |

Gold is number 79 on the Atomic Chart and has the symbol of Au and the Atomic Weight of 196.96655.

Written information could go here:
Gold is yellow in color and does not rust or tarnish.

Gold is inert to all pure acids. One troy ounce of gold can be drawn into a thin wire about 50 miles long.

One of the ways of finding gold is to pan for it.

Miners

More written information could go here:_____
_____
_____
_____

Gold has been found in United States, Canada, South Africa, and Russia.

Juan Trejo Per. 3

6. More Written information:
Include important facts.

7. Map or other graphic

8. Questions:
On bottom left of back side write 2 questions that can be answered by viewing your board.

9. Name:
Place your name in the lower right-hand corner.

From *Collaborative Library Research Projects: Inquiry that Stimulates the Senses* by John D. Volkman. Westport, CT: Libraries Unlimited. Copyright © 2008.

CHAPTER 15

Biography of Hispanic American Persons Brochure

Teacher Instructions

One of the assignments that the students find most enjoyable is the creation of a brochure highlighting the life of a famous Hispanic American. The research for this assignment requires the students to dive into the biographical reference books in the library. Armed with this information, as well as that gleaned from websites, the students have fun designing a brochure that highlights the life of their famous person.

The development of the assignment began with a discussion with the Chicano literature teacher about a creative way to research famous Hispanic Americans. The first step was to develop a list of important Hispanic Americans about whom there was information in the reference books. One of the primary goals of this lesson is to expose the students to the wealth of information available in the specialized biographical reference books.

The decision was then made to have the students develop a biographical brochure. Creating a brochure is a good way for students to summarize in a creative manner what they have learned. It is also a vehicle for sharing the information with the rest of the class.

The assignment is a prototype for creating similar projects on other types of biographical subjects. Simply use a different list of people and revise the list of specialized reference books to match the general subject being researched. The development of a brochure to share information is something that can be used for other types of assignments, such as travel brochures to highlight different geographical locations, scientific brochures to highlight scientific achievements or inventions, or historical brochures to spotlight events during a historical period.

The assignment is presented to the students in two parts. The first part is a sample brochure, which is set up so as include the directions and examples. The directions to the students on what information to include are printed in one font, and examples of this information are shown in another. The second part is a general bibliography of sources and a list of the Hispanic Americans to be studied.

MATERIALS NEEDED

1. *Encyclopedia of World Biography.* Farmington Hills, Mich.: Thompson-Gale, 1997. 2nd ed. 17 vols. $1375. 0–7876–2221–4. (Yearly supplement volumes since 1998: $150 each.)
2. Books with information on Hispanic Americans such as:

    -   *Contemporary Hispanic Biography.* Farmington Hills, Mich.: Thompson-Gale, 2003. 4 vols. $115 each. 0–7876–7151–7.
    -   Meyer, Nicholas E. *Biographical Dictionary of Hispanic Americans.* New York : Facts on File, 2001. 0–8160–4330–2.
    -   *Notable Hispanic American Women Book II.* Farmington Hills, Mich.: Thompson-Gale, 1998. 377p. $120. 0–7876–2068–8.

3. Wilson Biographies Plus Illustrated (http://vnweb.hwwilsonweb.com) and http://www.biography.com are good websites to use.
4. Note papers
5. Source pages with two books and two Internet sites, see Appendix 4.

UNIT CONSTRUCTION

1. Consult the reference books and websites to choose the persons to be studied.
2. Create a list of the people using a database such as Microsoft Excel. It is helpful to include the persons' professions so that students have an idea what type of specialized reference books to use.
3. Create Hispanic American Source List.

    -   List the general biography reference books and their call numbers.
    -   List the call numbers and categories of the specialized sets of reference books.
    -   List general subjects students can use in looking at the library catalog.
    -   List the Internet links such as Wilson Biographies Plus Illustrated (http://vnweb.hwwilsonweb.com) and http://www.biography.com and suggest the use of search engines.
    -   Paste the list of Hispanic Americans on the bottom or back of the source list.

4. Create a brochure/assignment sheet. Use different fonts to indicate which parts of the sheet are instructions and which parts are examples of what is required.
5. Print out the brochure/assignment sheets.

IN THE LIBRARY

1. Pass out the source pages and brochure/assignment sheets to the students.
2. Give everyone the yellow source page with two books and two Internet sources and a copy of the note paper.
3. Have plenty of source pages and note papers available.
4. Demonstrate to the students how to make brochures using Microsoft Word at the end of the last (second) day in the library.

    • Familiarize yourself with the directions for making brochures in Word.
    • Instruct the students to first type out their information in Word and then insert it into the brochure. It is much easier to manipulate that way rather than typing directly into the brochure.
    • Show students how to insert pictures, text blocks, and word art headings.

HISPANIC AMERICAN SOURCES

1. Start with *Reference (R)* Books.
2. *Encyclopedia of World Biography,* 19 vols., plus supplements
3. Hispanic American reference books such as:

   Contemporary Hispanic Biography
   Biographical Dictionary of Hispanic Americans
   Notable Hispanic American Women Book II

4. If your subject falls into a specific category, you can check specialized reference or regular nonfiction books in those categories such as the following:

364.9	Crime and Criminals
703	Art
781.66	Rock Music
791.43	Movies
791.45	Television
796	Sports Books
920.5	Scientists
920.8	Authors

5. Library catalog subjects:
   - Last name of your person to see if there is a biography of that person
   - Hispanic Americans

6. Internet:
   - Wilson Biographies Plus Illustrated (http://vnweb.hwwilsonweb.com)
   - http://www.biography.com/search/index.jsp
   - Search engines

HISPANIC AMERICANS

First Name	Last Name	Profession
Maria Conchita	Alonso	Actress
Julia	Alvarez	Author
Marc	Anthony	Singer
Desi	Arnaz	Actor
Judith E.	Baca	Artist
Joan	Baez	Singer
Ruben	Blades	Musician
Rod	Carew	Baseball
Mariah	Carey	Singer
Pablo	Casals	Artist
Julio "Cesar"	Chavez	Boxer
Evelyn	Cisneros	Dancer

Sandra	Cisneros	Author
Roberto	Clemente	Baseball
Oscar	de la Hoya	Boxer
Placido	Domingo	Musician
Hector	Elizondo	Actor
Jaime	Escalante	Teacher
Gloria	Esteban	Singer
Emilio	Estevez	Actor
Jose	Feliciano	Singer
Mary Joe	Fernandez	Tennis
Andy	Garcia	Actor
Dolores Fernandez	Huerta	Labor
Raul	Julia	Actor
Jennifer	Lopez	Actress
Nancy	Lopez	Golfer
Juan	Marichal	Baseball
Ricky	Martin	Singer
Nicholasa	Mohr	Author
Rita	Moreno	Actress
Edward James	Olmos	Actor
Jim	Plunkett	Football
Albert	Puljos	Baseball
Selena	Quintanilla-Perez	Singer
Bill	Richardson	Politician
Geraldo	Rivera	Newsman
Chi Chi	Rodriguez	Golfer
Paul M.	Rodriguez	Actor
Linda	Ronstadt	Singer
Alberto	Salazar	Runner
Ruben	Salazar	Journalist
Carlos	Santana	Musician
Juan	Serrano	Musician
Charlie	Sheen	Actor
Jimmy	Smits	Actor
Gary	Soto	Author
Piri	Thomas	Author
Lee	Trevino	Golfer
Luis	Valdez	Playwright
Ritchie	Valens	Singer
Fernando	Valenzuela	Baseball
Raquel	Welch	Actress

BIOGRAPHY OF HISPANIC PERSON, PAST OR PRESENT

PERSON: _____

16 Notes Due: _____

Brochure Due: _____

Assignment:

Your notable Hispanic person has been nominated to the Hall of Fame. In order to help have your person elected, you are going to create a brochure highlighting your person's life and accomplishments. A brochure consists of 6 sections. The sections should contain the following information about your person.

Front section: Title—In large letters, create a title using the name of the person and a picture.

Lee Trevino

Back section:

- Annotated Timeline showing 6-8 most important events and dates related to your person.
- Your name, date, period, class name
- Bibliography/Works Cited

Lee Trevino

--1939 Born

--1966 Earned PGA Tour card

--1968 Won U. S. Open at Oak Hill, NY

--1971 Won U. S. , British, & Canadian Opens

--1975 Struck by lighting

--1984 Won 2nd PGA Championship at age 44

--1990 Senior Tour Rookie and Player of the Year

Works Cited

Great Athletes. Pasadena: Salem Press, 2002.

Trevino, Lee (1939–). 2005. *GolfEurope.com.* Dec. 5, 2005. http://www.golfeurope.com/alman ac/players/trevino.htm.

Joan Jones
Dec. 18, 2007
Chicano Lit
Per. 5

1 section: Your personal opinion and analysis of your person

Lee Trevino never forgot his fatherless childhood and his humble beginnings. Though having only a seventh-grade education and being raised on bare floors with too little food and even less money, he proved that working hard one can accomplish his goals. He is a man who should be greatly admired for his attitude and work ethic.

He truly loves golf and has been a great ambassador for the sport. His quiet generosity to numerous charities where he demands complete confidentiality about his philanthropy is very admirable.

Trevino was known as the "Merry Mex."

Illustrations: Use 2 or more pictures or drawings highlighting person and/or events. **Captions:** Type appropriate captions to explain illustrations.

1 section: Basic Facts about person:

Birth

Death

Family

Where raised

Lee Trevino was raised in a run-down shack on the outskirts of Dallas. He only occasionally attended school in his early childhood. More often he helped his family by working in the dusty fields growing cotton and onions. An absent father was just one of the many hardships that Lee, his sisters, his mother, and his grandfather had to contend with.

1st Topic section:

Pick 2 of these topics and do 1 section on each:

- Education and training
- Road to fame
- Contributions to Hispanic Culture/Achievements
- Personality traits
- Disappointments in life or career
- Other people's opinion of this person
- Influence on society

Trevino had an awkward style that convinced some critics his stay on the tour would be a short one. Completely self-taught, Trevino's style was anything but smooth. During his swing he appeared to be frantically striving to retain his balance—however, at the critical moment when the face of the club strikes the ball, his body was perfectly coordinated. He did not take long to silence his critics, winning the U. S. Open in 1968 at Oak Hill. During the next six years he built a reputation as one of the game's stars. During a great four-week period in 1971 Trevino won three of golf's biggest tournaments in succession: U. S. Open, British Open, and Canadian Open.

Trevino's unique swing results in a consistent fade to each of his shots.

2nd Topic section:

Trevino is a surprisingly humble and private individual even though he has great humor and showmanship on the fairway. He is very generous to many charities perhaps due to his impoverished childhood. He uses humor to both ease the pressures of the game and to deflect prying eyes from his private life. He has the nickname of 'Supermex' and is one of golf's true heroes.

Research Requirements:

<u>Minimum:</u> 1 book and 1 Internet source

Grading:

1. 4 sections (paragraphs)	40	___
2. Notes (Minimum: 24)	20	___
3. 2 pictures	10	___
4. Creativity	10	___
5. Timeline	10	___
6. Bibliography	<u>10</u>	___
Total	100	___

From *Collaborative Library Research Projects: Inquiry that Stimulates the Senses* by John D. Volkman. Westport, CT: Libraries Unlimited. Copyright © 2008.

CHAPTER 16

Greek Heritage Essay/Poster and Newspaper

Teacher Instructions

The *Odyssey* and the *Iliad,* as well as *Oedipus Rex* and other Greek plays, are still read in classes everywhere. The reading of this classic literature provides a wonderful opportunity to study Greek culture, history, and heritage. With the wealth of information available and the importance of the Greek contributions, two projects are presented here. The first one is an essay/poster assignment and the second one is a newspaper creation.

The essay/poster is a basic way to study the cultural and historical information on the Greek civilization and is a good way for students to learn or practice their research and note-taking skills. The students also utilize the basic aspects of essay writing and citing sources in a bibliography.

The newspaper assignment is meant to be used with more advanced students and provide them the opportunity of exercising their creative skills in development of a newspaper-style end-product. The assignment includes many more topics than the poster assignment and challenges the students to use the information they glean in an original manner.

GREEK HERITAGE ESSAY/POSTER

Teacher Instructions

MATERIALS NEEDED

1. Books with information on Greek history and culture
2. Websites on Ancient Greece such as:
    http://www.historyforkids.org/learn/greeks/
    http://www.ancientgreece.com/
3. Note papers
4. Source pages with two books and two Internet sites, see Appendix 4

UNIT CONSTRUCTION

1. Put the books that have been pulled from the shelves on a book cart next to where the station is located. (Hint: Locating the station near the copier makes copying convenient and quicker.)
2. Alternatively, if time and class size make it feasible, students can find books using the library's catalog.
3. Put the suggested links on the library website.
4. Give everyone the yellow source page with two books and two Internet sources and a copy of the note paper.

GREEK HERITAGE

Essay/Poster Assignment

ASSIGNMENT

In order to better understand *The Odyssey,* we will be learning about ancient Greece, which was the birthplace of Western civilization. The awesome achievements of the ancient Greeks have left a heritage for science, government, philosophy, art, and much more.

You are to pretend that you are an imbedded reporter in ancient Greece. Each of you will investigate one of the topics below and write a two-page "feature article" describing your findings. You will also make a poster that you will use to briefly (3–5 minutes) tell the class about your topic. Your article should include details of the information illustrated on your poster. The article should be informative and written in proper essay form.

TOPICS

Government	Clothing
Athens	Olympics
Death	Philosophy
Religion/Gods	Pottery
Festivals	Farming/Fishing
Temples	Craftsmen
Homes	Science
Women	Medicine
Children	Education
Games	Coins/Money
Food	Land Warfare
Theater	Naval Warfare

POSTER BOARD CRITERIA

1   Size: 28" × 22"
2.   Contents:

   • Photos, drawings, cartoons, maps of pertinent people, events, places
   • Appropriate typed captions in your own words for each picture
   • Short, word-processed information describing topic

3.   On back side write two questions that your fellow students should be able to answer after viewing your board.

From *Collaborative Library Research Projects: Inquiry that Stimulates the Senses* by John D. Volkman. Westport, CT: Libraries Unlimited. Copyright © 2008.

GRADING

1. Essay (Final copy)   30 points   _____
2. First draft   10 points   _____
3. Poster   15 points   _____
4. Oral Report   15 points   _____
5. Note papers (minimum of 20)   20 points   _____
6. Bibliography/Works Cited   (10 points)
   - Sources all in one list alphabetically   2 points   _____
   - Book sources in proper form   4 points   _____
   - Internet sources in proper form   4 points   _____
7. Total   100 points   _____

RESEARCH STEPS/SOURCES

Day 1

Books

Library Catalog (General subjects to look up) Greece-Antiquities, Greece-History, 938 Books on Greece. (When you find a book, use the index to look up your topic).

At the end of the first period in the library, you must have at least eight notes from at least two sources with correct citation information recorded. You will have points deducted from "note papers" above if you do not.

Day 2

Internet

Use the Internet sites listed to find information on your topics: http://www.historyforkids.org/learn/greeks/; http://www.ancientgreece.com/. Use search engines to find more information.

At the end of the second period in the library, you must have at least 16 notes from at least two sources with correct citation information recorded. You will have points deducted from "note papers" above if you do not.

Poster Board Instructions

1. Size: 28" × 22"

2. Title: Place a title at the top using the name of your topic in large letters.

3. Pictures: Use photos or drawings of people, events, places.

4. Captions: Type appropriate captions for each picture.

GREEK PHILOSOPHY

Socrates developed the Socratic method based on questions and answers to find truth.

Written information could go here:_____
_____
_____

More written information could go here:_____
_____
_____
_____

An example of simple Greek philosophy would be the fables from Aesop, a Greek who told stories with morals to them. One of his fables is called "The Tortoise and the Hare."

Philosophy Started	Socrates Killed	Aristotle Born
500BC	399BC	384 BC

John Jones

5. Written information: Include important facts in brief, typed form.

6. Questions: On bottom left of back side write 2 questions that can be answered by viewing your board.

7. Timeline or chart: Show events or statistics in graphical form.

8. Name: Place your name in the lower right-hand corner.

From *Collaborative Library Research Projects: Inquiry that Stimulates the Senses* by John D. Volkman. Westport, CT: Libraries Unlimited. Copyright © 2008.

GREEK HERITAGE NEWSPAPER

Teacher Instructions

The newspaper assignment is a much more comprehensive assignment on the Greek heritage. It includes finding information on Greek mythology, famous Greeks, and important places in Greece, as well as Greek cultural topics. It is meant to be used with more advanced students who are capable of doing more extensive research and writing their information in a variety of newspaper-style formats.

Each of the students will have four different topics to research. They will then present them in at least six newspaper-style formats. To add an element of real newspaper reporting, the student submissions can be judged by the class or the teacher and the winning ones awarded "Pulitzer Prizes" such as candy bars, certificates, or other prizes.

MATERIALS NEEDED

1. Books with information on Greek history and culture
2. Books on Greek mythology
3. Websites on Ancient Greece such as:

    Ancient Greece: http://www.historyforkids.org/learn/greeks/
    Ancient Greece: http://www.ancientgreece.com/
    Greek mythology: http://homepage.mac.com/cparada/GML/
    Gods and myths: http://www.mythweb.com/
    Greek words, myths: http://library.oakland.edu/information/people/personal/
        kraemer/edcm/index.html
    Greek words: http://www.krysstal.com/borrow_greek.html
    Greek words: http://www.takeourword.com/theory.html
    Making Puzzles: http://puzzlemaker.school.discovery.com/chooseapuzzle.html

4. Note papers
5. Source pages for books (Appendix 1) and Internet (Appendix 2)

UNIT CONSTRUCTION

1. Provide examples of all the types of newspaper content that might be used.

    - Find an example of each of the "Types of Newspaper Content" listed under "Requirements" on the assignment sheet.
    - Make a one- or two-page collage of them with captions identifying them, and photocopy the collage.
    - Make copies of the pages for the students to see as examples so that they know about the many types of newspaper content.

2. Put the books that have been pulled from the shelves on a book cart next to where the station is located. (Hint: Locating the station near the copier makes copying convenient and quicker.)
3. Put the suggested links on the library website.
4. Give everyone the blue source page for books the first day.
5. Give everyone the green source page for Internet sources the second day.
6. Have plenty of source pages and note papers available.
7. Demonstrate to the students how to make columns using Microsoft Word (end of third day).

ANCIENT GREECE

Newspaper/Topics

ASSIGNMENT

In order to better understand *The Odyssey* we will be learning about ancient Greece, which was the birthplace of Western civilization. The awesome achievements of the ancient Greeks have left a heritage for science, government, philosophy, art, and much more.

You are to pretend that you are an imbedded reporter in ancient Greece. You are responsible for two pages of a newspaper. All of the sections from the class will be combined to form a comprehensive newspaper about Ancient Greece. Real journalists receive awards called "Pulitzer Prizes." Similarly, your sections will be judged by the class and the best ones will receive prizes.

REQUIREMENTS

1. You are to create a two-page newspaper that reports on topics and names related to ancient Greece.
2. Each of you will pick a row number from below and then create a newspaper that includes information about all of the subjects for that number: Topics, Gods/Heroes, Persons, and Places.
3. In your newspaper you will include the following *minimum* entries:

    A. One feature article—interesting, well-researched, creative, clear details, well-written
    B. One of the following: editorial, gossip column, interview, letter to editor, book review
    C. Two of the following: classified ads, obituaries, advertisements, comics
    D. Two of the following: maps, charts, pictures, weather
    E. Additional options that can be substituted for B–D above:

    - Have a section on vocabulary words derived from Greek. See websites for information.
    - Rewrite a Greek myth from the point of view of a reporter, telling the myth as a news event.
    - Make a puzzle using Odyssey/Mythology/Ancient Greece-related terms. See *Puzzlemaker* website for ideas.
    - Describe or draw a constellation and write a horoscope related to it.
    - You may make multiple entries for your topics.

4. Just as real reporters do, you must record your findings using the note papers.
5. You need to use a book and an Internet source with a minimum of eight notes on each topic.
6. Pictures should have captions.
7. Stories and articles should have headlines.

From *Collaborative Library Research Projects: Inquiry that Stimulates the Senses* by John D. Volkman. Westport, CT: Libraries Unlimited. Copyright © 2008.

TOPICS

Choose one of the numbered rows below:

Topics	Gods/Heroes	Persons	Places
1. Government	Aphrodite	Solon	Acropolis
2. Death	Apollo	Achilles	Hades
3. Warfare	Ares	Alexander	Sparta
4. Festivals	Artemis	Euripides	Thrace
5. Temples	Athena	Sophocles	Athens
6. Homes	Demeter	Oedipus	Thebes
7. Women	Dionysus	Hercules	Pompeii
8. Children	Hades	Aristotle	Delphi
9. Games	Hephaestus	Epicurus	Crete
10. Food	Hera	Plato	Corinth
11. Theater	Hermes	Aesop	Knossos
12. Clothing	Harpies	Homer	Epidaurus
13. Olympics	Persephone	Plutarch	Olympia
14. Philosophy	Poseidon	Socrates	Mycenae
15. Pottery	Zeus	Archimedes	Marathon
16. Farming/Fishing	Atlas	Euclid	Troy
17. Craftsmen	Calypso	Hector	Macedonia
18. Science	Prometheus	Ptolemy	Thermopylae
19. Medicine	Pandora	Hippocrates	Salamis
20. Education	Pan	Pythagoras	Parthenon

RESEARCH STEPS/SOURCES

Day 1

Library Catalog (General subjects to look up)

Greece-Antiquities

Greece-History

Mythology

At the end of the first period in the library, you must have at least eight notes on at least two topics done with their book sources properly recorded. You will have points deducted from "note papers" above if you do not.

Day 2

Internet

Websites on Ancient Greece:

Ancient Greece: http://www.historyforkids. org/learn/greeks/

Ancient Greece: http://www.ancientgreece. com/

Greek mythology: http://homepage.mac. com/cparada/GML/

Gods and myths: http://www.mythweb.com/

Greek words, myths: http://library.oakland. edu/information/people/personal/kraemer/ edcm/index.html

Greek words: http://www.krysstal.com/ bor row_greek.html

Greek words: http://www.takeourword.com/ theory.html

Making Puzzles: http://puzzlemaker.school. discovery.com/chooseapuzzle.html

Use search engines to find more information.

At the end of the second period in the library, you must have at least 16 notes done, including 8 with their Internet sources properly recorded. You will have points deducted from "note papers" above if you do not.

Day 3

Book or Internet

Find more information on the topics.

Minimum of eight more note papers.

Instruction in creating columns and inserting pictures in Microsoft Word (last part of the period).

GRADING

1.	One feature article	50 points	_____
2.	Editorial, gossip column, interview, letter to editor, book review	30 points	_____
3.	Classified ads, obituaries, advertisements, comics	25 points	_____
4.	Maps, charts, pictures, weather	25 points	_____
5.	Note papers (minimum of 32)	32 points	_____
6.	Layout	20 points	_____
7.	Spelling and proofreading	8 points	_____
8.	Bibliography/Works Cited	(10 points)	
	• Sources all in one list alphabetically	2 points	_____
	• Book sources in proper form	4 points	_____
	• Internet sources in proper form	4 points	_____
9.	Total	200 points	_____

CHAPTER 17

Shoebox Float Project: The Nations of the World Report

Teacher Instructions

The shoebox float project is a five-part project devoted to investigating and reporting on one of the countries of the world. It begins with the students choosing one of the countries of the world and writing a letter to its embassy requesting information. It continues with the students delving into a variety of print and nonprint resources to find information about their country and producing two library research worksheets. Students then use the information gathered to write an individual research paper.

For the last part of the assignment, students are combined into groups. Each group builds a shoebox float highlighting their country. The groups make an oral presentation to the class explaining their shoebox and highlighting their country. Additionally, all of the shoeboxes are put on display in the library or other prominent place. This "Parade of Countries" is judged to determine the best floats and highest grades.

INSTRUCTIONS TO GIVE TO THE STUDENTS

The shoebox float project is designed to be a semester-long, ongoing project that the students work on periodically as they continue to do their other classroom work.

Therefore, the timeline proposed below covers about a four-month period. Certainly, it can be condensed to fit other time schedules.

Explain the assignment to the students at the beginning of the semester. The letter to the embassy should be written in the first three weeks of the semester and mailed out in the first month to insure plenty of time for receiving information back. The first library research assignment should be done about six weeks into the grading period with the second one due a month later. The research paper done using the information gleaned can then be due the following month. The students work in their country groups (three students per country is the optimum number) and present their shoeboxes the next month.

Roger Hoeflinger is the world cultures teacher who collaborated in developing this shoebox float project. He had this to say about the project:

For the past five years, I have ended the school year in World Cultures with a special unit called "Country Shoebox Float." I got the idea from my own experience in fifth grade. We were studying the states in Geography, and my partner and I had to do our shoebox float on the state of Arkansas.

When our high school started giving the STAR test a few years ago, we discovered that all of our curriculum needed to be covered in class by April or the students would not do very well on the test. Left with five to six weeks at the end of the year to compare and contrast the different countries of the modern post-war world, I decided to try the Shoebox Float Project. There are very few questions on the STAR test from this unit, outside of the Cold War, so I decided to teach up through the Cold War before the STAR test and use this project in the last six weeks of school to teach about the different countries of the world.

One of the benefits of this idea was that it got us out of the traditional textbook and into the library to do the research. Our librarian was a tremendous help. He developed all of the research worksheets and source lists and he basically teaches a mini-unit on research as we begin the unit. We spend four to five days in the library with each class on research, and then the students work in groups of three to complete the floats and give oral presentations to their class.

Part of the project uses cooperative learning, and part uses individual research, as well as traditional teaching methods. Academic rigor is accomplished through the research paper which accompanies the float. It must be done individually, not in the group.

I have been very pleased with the outcome of this project. Every year it is amazing to see the artistic expression and creativity displayed by students at all levels and the obvious learning that is being accomplished. It has been a great way to end the school year.

SHOEBOX FLOAT PROJECT

THE NATIONS OF THE WORLD REPORT

There are close to 200 independent nations in the world. Each of you will be doing extensive library research about your country. You will learn to use a variety of library reference book sources and Internet websites. With the information gleaned, you will write a research paper on your country. With the other students who have the same country as you do, you will build a shoebox float highlighting your country and present it to the class.

ASSIGNMENT

There are five parts to this assignment; the first four are individual and the last one is done in a group.

1. Written letter to the nation's embassy
2. "Countries of the World" library worksheet
3. "Country Information Page" library worksheet
4. Written research paper of three to five pages
5. Shoebox float with an oral presentation to the class

LETTER TO THE NATION'S EMBASSY

1. Write a letter to the nation's embassy. In the letter, ask for information that would be useful in writing a research paper and in making an oral presentation.
2. The letter must be in proper formal letter block style.
3. Find the address to the embassy in an almanac.
4. The letter must be approved by the teacher as being acceptable in order to receive credit. Unacceptable letters must be redone until they are correct.
5. Each group of three students will choose the letter they wish to send to the embassy from among their three letters.

   • The rough draft copy is due to me on _____
   • The final correct copy is due to me on _____
   • The letter must be in the mail by _____
   • Total points: **50.**

LIBRARY RESEARCH ASSIGNMENTS

1. "Countries-Sources" Worksheet

   • One class period in the library; finish on your own time.
   • Due: _____ Total points: **50.**

2. "Country Information Page" worksheet.

   • To be done on your own time in the Library.
   • Due: _____ Total points: **50.**

RESEARCH PAPER ASSIGNMENT

- Written research paper of three to five pages on country
- Fulfill the detailed requirements on the "Country Report" instruction page.
- Due: _____ Total points: **100.**

GRADING

1.	Letter to the nation's embassy	50 points	_____
2.	Country sources worksheet	50 points	_____
3.	Country information worksheet	50 points	_____
4.	Research paper	100 points	_____
5.	Shoebox float	100 points	_____
6.	Oral presentation	50 points	_____
7.	Country sources worksheet	50 points	_____
8.	Total	450 points	_____

COUNTRIES--SOURCES

COUNTRY:_____

1. Look up the subject: **COUNTRIES—ENCYCLOPEDIAS** in the library catalog. Write down the call number of one of the books and then find the book on the shelf. After you find the book, look at the title page and the back of it (for date) and write the following information about the book:

_____ . _____

AUTHOR (OR EDITOR)   TITLE of BOOK

_____ . _____ :

PLACE

_____ , _____ . PAGES USED: _____ .

PUBLISHER   YEAR PUBLISHED

Call Number
_____
_____
_____

Write down 5 notes or facts about your country from the book. Be sure they are phrases, not sentences. Include the page you found the information on.

p._____ _____

p._____ _____

p._____ _____

p._____ _____

p._____ _____

2. Look up the name of your country in the library catalog. Find a **nonfiction book** (one that has a Dewey Decimal Number) that is "IN." (If there is not a book on your country, use another reference book.) Write down the call number of the book and then find the book on the shelf. After you find the book, look at the title page and the back of it (for date) and write the following information about the book:

_____ . _____

AUTHOR (OR EDITOR)   TITLE of BOOK

_____ . _____ :

PLACE

_____ , _____ . PAGES USED: _____ .

PUBLISHER   YEAR PUBLISHED

Call Number
_____
_____
_____

Write down 5 notes or facts from the book. Be sure they are phrases, not sentences. Include the page you found the information on.

p._____ _____

p._____ _____

p._____ _____

p._____ _____

p._____ _____

3. Look up the subject: **ALMANACS** in the library catalog. Write down the call number of one of the books and then find the book on the shelf. After you find the book, look at the title page and the back of it (for copyright date) and write the following information about the book:

Call Number
_____
_____
_____

_____ . _____
AUTHOR (OR EDITOR)   TITLE of BOOK

_____ . _____ :
                                              PLACE

_____ , _____ . PAGES USED: _____ .
PUBLISHER   YEAR PUBLISHED

Write down 5 notes or facts from the book. Be sure they are phrases, not sentences. Include the page you found the information on.

p._____ _____

p._____ _____

p._____ _____

p._____ _____

p._____ _____

4. Look up the subject: **ATLASES** in the library catalog. Write down the call number of one of the books and then find the book on the shelf or on the atlas stand. After you find the book, look at the title page and the back of it (for copyright date) and write the following information about the book:

Call Number
_____
_____
_____

_____ . _____
AUTHOR (OR EDITOR)   TITLE of BOOK

_____ . _____ :
                                              PLACE

_____ , _____ . PAGES USED: _____ .
PUBLISHER   YEAR PUBLISHED

Use the atlas to draw your map on the last page.

5. Packet from the letter you wrote to your embassy .

_____ . _____
NAME OF EMBASSY   TITLE

_____ . _____ , _____ .
                                              PLACE   DATE

Embassy of Serbia and Montenegro. *Information Packet.* Washington, D.C., 2005

6. Use one of these websites:

Background Notes - http://www.state.gov/r/pa/ei/bgn/
CIA World Fact Book - https://www.cia.gov/library/publications/the-world-factbook/index.html
Visual Geography Series - http://www.vgsbooks.com/

Write down the bibliographic information about your Internet source in the section below:

WEBSITE

AUTHOR (IF GIVEN)	NAME OF WEB PAGE OR ARTICLE
DATE OF POSTING/REVISION	NAME OF ORGANIZATION AFFILIATED WITH SITE
DATE YOU READ IT	ELECTRONIC ADDRESS (URL)

Write down 5 notes or facts from the site. Be sure they are phrases, not sentences.

_____
_____
_____
_____
_____

7. Use a periodical database to find a magazine or newspaper article.

Write down the bibliographic information about your Internet source in the section below:

PERIODICAL

AUTHOR (IF GIVEN)	NAME OF ARTICLE	
NAME OF PERIODICAL	DATE OF PERIODICAL	NAME OF DATABASE SOURCE
DATE YOU READ IT	ELECTRONIC ADDRESS (URL)	

Write down 3–5 notes or facts from the site. Be sure they are phrases, not sentences.

_____
_____
_____
_____
_____

Draw a map of your country in the box below. Make sure you label the country, its capital, and the countries that surround it. Also make a Xerox copy of a map for future use and staple it to the back of this assignment.

Legend

Find and write down the following about your country's capital city:

Name of capital:_____

Latitude:_____

Longitude:_____

Name _____

Date _____ Per. _____

Teacher _____

Country Information Page

General Information:

Formal Name:_____, (Source # _____ Page # _____)

Name of Capital City:_____, (Source # _____ Page # _____)

    Latitude:_____, (Source # _____ Page # _____)

    Longitude: _____, (Source # _____ Page # _____)

Name of Citizen:_____, (Source # _____ Page # _____)

National Holidays:_____ , _____ ,

_____ , _____ ,(Source # _____ Page # _____)

Government:

Form of Government: _____ , (Source # _____ Page # _____)

Name and Title of Current Head of Government: _____

_____ , (Source # _____ Page # _____)

Land and Location:

Area: _____ , (Source # _____ Page # _____)

Major Cities: _____

_____

_____ , (Source # _____ Page # _____)

Topography: _____

_____ , (Source # _____ Page # _____)

Climate: _____

_____

_____ , (Source # _____ Page # _____)

Natural Resources: _____

_____

_____ , (Source # _____ Page # _____)

Time: _____ = noon Greenwich Mean Time (GMT), (Source # _____ Page # _____)

Time Zone your country is in: _____ , (Source # _____ Page # _____)

From *Collaborative Library Research Projects: Inquiry that Stimulates the Senses* by John D. Volkman. Westport, CT: Libraries Unlimited. Copyright © 2008.

Economy:

Main industries: _____

_____

_____ , (Source # _____ Page # _____)

Major Agricultural Products: _____

_____

_____ , (Source # _____ Page # _____)

Currency Name/Value in Dollars: _____ ,

_____ ,(Source # _____ Page # _____)

Major services: _____ ,

_____ ,(Source # _____ Page # _____)

Major imports: _____ ,

_____ ,(Source # _____ Page # _____)

Major exports: _____ ,

_____ ,(Source # _____ Page # _____)

Current Gross Domestic Product: $_____ ,(Source # _____ Page # _____)

Current GDP per capita: $_____ , (Source # _____ Page # _____)

People:

Population: _____ , (Source # _____ Page # _____)

Population density: _____ per square kilometer , (Source # _____ Page # _____)

Life Expectancy: Males_____ years,   (Source # _____ Page # _____)

Life Expectancy: Females_____ years,   (Source # _____ Page # _____)

Ethnic groups: _____ , _____

_____ , _____ , _____

_____ , (Source # _____ Page # _____)

Literacy Rate: _____ %   (Source # _____ Page # _____)

Official Language: _____ , (Source # _____ Page # _____)

Other Major Languages: _____ , _____

_____ , _____ , _____

_____ , (Source # _____ Page # _____)

Major Religions: _____ , _____

_____ , _____ , _____

_____ , (Source # _____ Page # _____)

From *Collaborative Library Research Projects: Inquiry that Stimulates the Senses* by John D. Volkman. Westport, CT: Libraries Unlimited. Copyright © 2008.

Famous people: _____

_____

_____ , (Source # _____ Page # _____)

History, Current Events:

Major facts or events: _____

_____

_____ , (Source # _____ Page # _____)

Major facts or events: _____

_____

_____ , (Source # _____ Page # _____)

Major facts or events: _____

_____

_____ , (Source # _____ Page # _____)

Major facts or events: _____

_____

_____ , (Source # _____ Page # _____)

Historical Places/Museums: _____

_____

_____ , (Source # _____ Page # _____)

Drawing or picture of the nation's flag:	Drawing or picture of the nation's seal:
(Source # _____ Page # _____)	(Source # _____ Page # _____)

From *Collaborative Library Research Projects: Inquiry that Stimulates the Senses* by John D. Volkman. Westport, CT: Libraries Unlimited. Copyright © 2008.

Country Report

You have gathered a large amount of information about your country as you have done your library research worksheets. The next step is to use that information to write a report about your country. In writing the paper, be sure to include all of the required elements as outlined below.

INFORMATION TO INCLUDE

1. Geographical and physical description of the country
2. History of nation starting after 1492 and ending at current year
3. Description of the country's people and their way of life
4. Description of the current government (post-2000)
5. Timeline: History of the nation from 1492 to current year

APPENDICES

1. Current physical map
2. Current political map
3. Picture or drawing of country's flag, in color
4. Picture or drawing of national seal, in color
5. Copy of letter sent to your country's embassy

STRUCTURE OF THE PAPER

1. Three- to five-page report
2. Word-processed: Double-spaced and Times New Roman, size 12 font
3. All quotes or extracts in proper format
4. Title page
5. Table of contents
6. Bibliography/Works Cited
7. Minimum of five sources including at least two books and two from the Internet

GRADING

1.	Information (3–5 page final copy)	50 points	_____
2.	Appendices	(25 points)	_____
	• Current physical map	5 points	_____
	• Current political map	5 points	_____
	• Picture or drawing of country's flag, in color	5 points	_____
	• Picture or drawing of national seal, in color	5 points	_____
	• Copy of letter sent to your country's embassy	5 points	_____
3.	Structure	15 points	_____

From *Collaborative Library Research Projects: Inquiry that Stimulates the Senses* by John D. Volkman. Westport, CT: Libraries Unlimited. Copyright © 2008.

4. Bibliography/Works Cited   (10 points)
   - Sources all in one list alphabetically   2 points   _____
   - Book sources in proper form   4 points   _____
   - Internet sources in proper form   4 points   _____
5. Total   100 points   _____

   Due: _____

Shoebox Parade Float and Oral Presentation

SHOEBOX FLOAT REQUIREMENTS

1. Shoebox as its base (no boot boxes)
2. Rolling wheels
3. Name of the country prominently displayed on the float
4. Depict things about the nation such as:

- Flag
- Seal
- Bird
- Symbol
- Traditions/culture
- Dress

- Religions
- History
- Geographical features
- Other things that are interesting or unique

ORAL PRESENTATION REQUIREMENTS

1. Five-minute oral presentation about your nation
2. Explain each part of the float and give a brief overview of your nation.
3. All three members of the group must participate, including speaking.

ORAL PRESENTATIONS WILL BE ON THE FOLLOWING DAYS

Total points

Shoebox float: **100 points**
Oral presentation: **50 points**

Shoebox Parade

1. The floats will be put on display in the library.
2. A group of teachers will judge them and the winning float in each class will receive *50 extra credit points* for each member of the group.
3. The grand champion of all six classes will also receive an *extra 50 points*.
4. Judging will be based on the following criteria:

- The requirements for a shoebox floated listed above
- Creativity
- Originality

- Decorative/artistic qualities
- Informativeness
- Overall impression

Each student is responsible for helping in the construction of the float and in making the oral presentation of the shoebox float to the class.

From *Collaborative Library Research Projects: Inquiry that Stimulates the Senses* by John D. Volkman. Westport, CT: Libraries Unlimited. Copyright © 2008.

Countries of the World by Continent

Asia

Afghanistan
Bahrain
Bangladesh
Bhutan
India
Iran
Israel
Japan
Jordan
Kazakhstan
Kuwait
Kyrgyzstan
Lebanon
Maldives
Mongolia
Nepal
North Korea
Oman
Pakistan
Peoples Republic of China
Qatar
Saudi Arabia
South Korea
Sri Lanka
Syria
Taiwan (Republic of China)
Tajikistan
Turkey
Turkmenistan
United Arab Emirates
Uzbekistan
Yemen

Africa

Algeria
Angola
Benin
Botswana
Burkina Faso
Burundi
Cameroon
Cape Verde
Central African Republic
Chad
Comoros
Congo
Democratic Republic of the Congo (Zaire)
Djibouti
Egypt
Equatorial Guinea
Eritrea
Ethiopia
The Gambia
Ghana
Guinea
Guinea-Bissau
Ivory Coast (Côte d'Ivoire)
Kenya
Lesotho
Liberia
Madagascar
Malawi
Malaysia
Mali
Mauritania
Mauritius
Morocco
Mozambique
Namibia
Niger
Rwanda
Sao Tome and Principe
Senegal
Seychelles
Sierra Leone
Somalia
South Africa
Sudan
Swaziland
Tanzania
Togo
Tunisia
Uganda
Western Sahara
Zambia
Zimbabwe

Europe

Albania
Andorra
Armenia
Austria
Azerbaijan
Belarus
Belgium
Bosnia and Herzegovina
Bulgaria
Croatia
Cyprus
Czech Republic
Denmark
England
Estonia
Finland
France
Georgia
Germany
Greece
Hungary
Iceland
Ireland
Italy
Latvia
Liechtenstein
Luxembourg
Macedonia
Malta
Moldova
Monaco
Netherlands
Norway
Poland
Portugal
Romania
Russia
San Marino
Scotland
Slovakia
Slovenia
Spain
Sweden
Switzerland
Ukraine
Wales
Vatican City
Yugoslavia

North America and the Caribbean

Antigua and Barbuda
The Bahamas
Barbados
Belize
Canada
Cuba
Dominica
Dominican Republic
Grenada
Haiti
Jamaica
Kalaallit Nunaat
    (formerly Greenland)
Mexico
Saint Lucia
Saint Vincent and the Grenadines
Saint Kitts and Nevis
Trinidad and Tobago

South and Central America

Argentina
Belize
Bolivia
Brazil
Chile
Colombia
Costa Rica
Ecuador
El Salvador
French Guiana
Guatemala
Guyana
Honduras
Nicaragua
Panama
Paraguay
Peru
Suriname
Uruguay
Venezuela

Southeast Asia and Oceania

Australia
Brunei
Cambodia
East Timor
Federated States of Micronesia
Fiji
Indonesia
Laos
Malaysia
Marshall Islands
Myanmar (formerly Burma)
Nauru
New Zealand
Palau
Papua New Guinea
Philippines
Solomon Islands
Tonga
Tuvalu
Samoa
Singapore
Thailand
Vietnam

JUDGING SCORE SHEET FOR SHOEBOX FLOAT CONTEST

Country _____ Period _____ Student 1_____

Student 2_____ Student 3_____

1. It has rolling wheels.

No			Wheels but don't turn					Yes	
1	2	3	4	5	6	7	8	9	10

2. It depicts things about the nation such as flag, seal, bird, products, dress, religions, history, geography, map, culture, etc.

None				Few				Many	
1	2	3	4	5	6	7	8	9	10

No Evidence				Average				Excellent	

3. It is built from a shoebox base.

1	2	3	4	5	6	7	8	9	10

4. Creativity.

1	2	3	4	5	6	7	8	9	10

5. Originality.

1	2	3	4	5	6	7	8	9	10

6. Decorative/Artistic.

1	2	3	4	5	6	7	8	9	10

7. Informative.

1	2	3	4	5	6	7	8	9	10

8. Overall Impression.

1	2	3	4	5	6	7	8	9	10

TOTAL (80) _____ SIGNATURE OF JUDGE _____

Appendixes

BIBLIOGRAPHY/WORKS CITED

General Rules

1. Alphabetize entries by author's last name. If there is no author, use the first word of the title (skip A, An, The).
2. Titles are italicized.
3. Double space all lines.
4. Begin each entry at the left margin (1″) and indent subsequent lines five spaces from the margin.
5. Each period is followed by one space. Each colon is followed by one space.
6. Center the title Works Cited one inch from the top. Double-space before the first entry.

Basic Book Format:	Author(s). *Title of Book.* Place of Publication: Publisher, Year of Publication.
Book by single author	Morris, Randy. *Big Book of Dogs.* Chicago: Knopf, 2007.
Book by two or three authors	Berry, Jason and Norman Patch. *Life Among the Thorns.* New York: Watts, 2003.
Book with an editor	Kunitz, Stanley J., ed. *American Authors, 1600–1900.* New York: H. W. Wilson, 1938.
Encyclopedia (Signed)	Asimov, Issac. "Meteor." *World Book Encyclopedia.* 2005.
Encyclopedia (Unsigned)	"Baseball." *Encyclopedia Americana.* 2005.
Basic Periodical:	Author(s). "Title of Article." *Title of Source.* Month Day, Year: pages.
Magazine	Phoenix, Brooke. "River of No Return." *People Weekly.* Nov. 30, 2003: 42–45.
Newspaper	Holmes, Sonny. "Study Sees Solar Heat for Houses." *Fresno Bee.* Mar. 10, 2004: A1.
Pamphlet	Cohn, Anne H. *Physical Child Abuse.* Chicago: National Committee for Child Abuse, 2003. (Treat the same as a book).
Basic Internet Source:	Author(s). Name of Webpage. Date of Posting/Revision. Name of organization affiliated with the site. electronic address (URL).Accessed Date you read it.

Website	Maxwell, Jill. *Elizabethan Sports.* Dec. 17, 1999. Purdue University. http://omni.cc.purdue.edu/Efelluga/theory2.html. Accessed Nov. 15, 2004.
Electronic Database (Proquest, Infotrac, SIRS, Lexis-Nexis, etc.)	Russell, Michael. "The Great Debate." *Glamour. Proquest,* Jan. 1995: l78–83. Accessed Dec. 1999.
	Frick, Robert. "Investing in Medical Miracles." *Kiplinger's.*
	Feb. 1999: 80–87. *SIRS Researcher.* Feb. 25, 2004. http://www.sirs.com.
Other Media:	Author's name, last name first (if available). "Article or web page title." *Website title.* URL. Access date, City: Producer. [city and producer are optional]
Online Encyclopedia	Beasley, Maurine H. "Roosevelt, Eleanor." *WorldBook Online,* 2007. http://www.worldbookonline.com. Accessed May 3, 2007.
Interview	Crawford, Mark. Personal Interview. Apr. 3, 2007.
Television or radio	"The Present." Narr. Morley Safer. *Sixty Minutes.* CBS. KJEO, Fresno. Accessed May 19, 2005.
Videotape	*Civil War Diary.* Videotape. World Studio, 1990.

SAMPLE WORKS CITED

Asimov, Isaac. "Meteor." *World Book Encyclopedia.* 2005.

"Baseball." *Encyclopedia Americana.* 2005.

Berry, Jason, and Norman Patch. *Life Among the Thorns.* New York: Watts, 2003.

"How to Train Picky Eaters." *Parents.* May 2002, 9–10.

Kunitz, Stanley J., ed. *American Authors, 1600-1900.* New York: H. W. Wilson, 1938.

Maxwell, Jill. *Elizabethan Sports.* Dec.17, 1999. Purdue University. http://omni.cc.purdue.edu/Efelluga/theory2.html. Accessed Nov. 15, 2004

Morris, Randy. *Big Book of Dogs.* Chicago: Knopf, 2004.

Phoenix, Brooke. "River of No Return." *People Weekly.* November 30, 2003, 42–45.

"The Present." Narr. Morley Safer. *Sixty Minutes.* CBS. KJEO, Fresno, Calif.. May 19, 2005.

Russell, Michael. "The Great Debate." *Glamour.* EBSCO, Jan. 1995: l78–83. Accessed Dec. 1999.

Note for web sources: It is necessary to list your date of access because web postings are often updated, and information available at one date may no longer be available later. Be sure to include the complete address for the site.

There are many websites to help with bibliography. They include the following:

http://www.easybib.com

http://www.noodletools.com

http://www.frsd.k12.nj.us/copperlibrary/student/sbib.html

BLUE

NAME: _____

TEACHER: _____

DATE: _____ PER.: _____

SOURCE PAGE—Books

1. _____ . _____
   AUTHOR (OR EDITOR)   TITLE of BOOK

   _____ . _____ :
                                      PLACE

   _____ , _____ . PAGES USED: _____ .
   PUBLISHER   YEAR PUBLISHED

Call Number
_____
_____
_____

2. _____ . _____
   AUTHOR (OR EDITOR)   TITLE of BOOK

   _____ . _____ :
                                      PLACE

   _____ , _____ . PAGES USED: _____ .
   PUBLISHER   YEAR PUBLISHED

Call Number
_____
_____
_____

3. _____ . _____
   AUTHOR (OR EDITOR)   TITLE of BOOK

   _____ . _____ :
                                      PLACE

   _____ , _____ . PAGES USED: _____ .
                            YEAR PUBLISHED

Call Number
_____
_____
_____

4. _____ . _____
   AUTHOR (OR EDITOR)   TITLE of BOOK

   _____ . _____ :
                                      PLACE

   _____ , _____ . PAGES USED: _____ .
   PUBLISHER   YEAR PUBLISHED

Call Number
_____
_____
_____

5. _____ . _____
   AUTHOR (OR EDITOR)   TITLE of BOOK

   _____ . _____ :
                                      PLACE

   _____ , _____ . PAGES USED: _____ .
   PUBLISHER   YEAR PUBLISHED

Call Number
_____
_____
_____

BIBLIOGRAPHIC EXAMPLE:

Author(s). *Title of Book*. Place of Publication: Publisher, Year of Publication.

Avila, Martin. *Living With Books*. New York: Forest Press, 2003.

GREEN

NAME: _____

TEACHER: _____

DATE: _____ PER.: _____

SOURCE PAGE—Internet Websites

1. _____ . _____ .
   AUTHOR (IF GIVEN)   NAME OF WEB PAGE OR ARTICLE

   _____ . _____
   DATE OF POSTING/REVISION   NAME OF ORGANIZATION AFFILIATED WITH SITE

   _____ . _____ .
   ELECTRONIC ADDRESS (URL)   DATE YOU READ IT

2. _____ . _____ .
   AUTHOR (IF GIVEN)   NAME OF WEB PAGE OR ARTICLE

   _____ . _____
   DATE OF POSTING/REVISION   NAME OF ORGANIZATION AFFILIATED WITH SITE

   _____ . _____ .
   ELECTRONIC ADDRESS (URL)   DATE YOU READ IT

3. _____ . _____ .
   AUTHOR (IF GIVEN)   NAME OF WEB PAGE OR ARTICLE

   _____ . _____
   DATE OF POSTING/REVISION   NAME OF ORGANIZATION AFFILIATED WITH SITE

   _____ . _____ .
   ELECTRONIC ADDRESS (URL)   DATE YOU READ IT

4. _____ . _____ .
   AUTHOR (IF GIVEN)   NAME OF WEB PAGE OR ARTICLE

   _____ . _____
   DATE OF POSTING/REVISION   NAME OF ORGANIZATION AFFILIATED WITH SITE

   _____ . _____ .
   ELECTRONIC ADDRESS (URL)   DATE YOU READ IT

5. _____ . _____ .
   AUTHOR (IF GIVEN)   NAME OF WEB PAGE OR ARTICLE

   _____ . _____
   DATE OF POSTING/REVISION   NAME OF ORGANIZATION AFFILIATED WITH SITE

   _____ . _____ .
   ELECTRONIC ADDRESS (URL)   DATE YOU READ IT

EXAMPLE:

Author. Name of Web page or Article. Date of Posting/Revision. Name of Organization Affiliated with Site. Electronic Address (URL). Date You Read It.

Maxwell, Jill. "Crime and Punishment in Elizabethan England." April 3, 2001. *EyeWitness to History*. April 15, 2005. http://www.eyewitnesstohistory.com.

PINK

NAME: _____

TEACHER: _____

DATE: _____ PER.: _____

SOURCE PAGE—Periodicals

1. _____ . _____ .
   AUTHOR (IF GIVEN)   NAME OF ARTICLE

   _____ . _____ : _____ . _____ .
   NAME OF PERIODICAL (SOURCE)   DATE   PAGES   NAME OF DATABASE SOURCE

   _____ . _____ .
   ELECTRONIC ADDRESS (URL)   DATE YOU READ IT

2. _____ . _____ .
   AUTHOR (IF GIVEN)   NAME OF ARTICLE

   _____ . _____ : _____ . _____ .
   NAME OF PERIODICAL (SOURCE)   DATE   PAGES   NAME OF DATABASE SOURCE

   _____ . _____ .
   ELECTRONIC ADDRESS (URL)   DATE YOU READ IT

3. _____ . _____ .
   AUTHOR (IF GIVEN)   NAME OF ARTICLE

   _____ . _____ : _____ . _____ .
   NAME OF PERIODICAL (SOURCE)   DATE   PAGES   NAME OF DATABASE SOURCE

   _____ . _____ .
   ELECTRONIC ADDRESS (URL)   DATE YOU READ IT

4. _____ . _____ .
   AUTHOR (IF GIVEN)   NAME OF ARTICLE

   _____ . _____ : _____ . _____ .
   NAME OF PERIODICAL (SOURCE)   DATE   PAGES   NAME OF DATABASE SOURCE

   _____ . _____ .
   ELECTRONIC ADDRESS (URL)   DATE YOU READ IT

5. _____ . _____ .
   AUTHOR (IF GIVEN)   NAME OF ARTICLE

   _____ . _____ : _____ . _____ .
   NAME OF PERIODICAL (SOURCE)   DATE   PAGES   NAME OF DATABASE SOURCE

   _____ . _____ .
   ELECTRONIC ADDRESS (URL)   DATE YOU READ IT

EXAMPLE:

Author's name. "Title of the Article." *Original Source of Article.* Date of original source: page numbers. *Name of the Database Used.* URL of service's homepage. Date of access.

Frick, Robert. "Investing in Medical Miracles." *Kiplinger's Personal Finance* Feb. 1999:80-87. *SIRS Researcher.* http://www.sirs.com. Feb. 25, 2004.

YELLOW

NAME: _____

TEACHER: _____

DATE: _____ PER.: _____

SOURCE PAGE—Books and Internet

BOOK

1. _____ . _____   Call Number
   AUTHOR (OR EDITOR)   TITLE of BOOK

   _____ . _____ :   _____
                                        PLACE   _____

   _____ , _____ . PAGES USED: _____ .   _____
   PUBLISHER   YEAR PUBLISHED

BOOK

2. _____ . _____   Call Number
   AUTHOR (OR EDITOR)   TITLE of BOOK

   _____ . _____ :   _____
                                        PLACE   _____

   _____ , _____ . PAGES USED: _____ .   _____
   PUBLISHER   YEAR PUBLISHED

WEBSITE

3. _____ . _____ .
   AUTHOR (IF GIVEN)   NAME OF WEB PAGE OR ARTICLE

   _____ . _____
   DATE OF POSTING/REVISION NAME OF ORGANIZATION AFFILIATED WITH SITE

   _____ . _____ .
   ELECTRONIC ADDRESS (URL)   DATE YOU READ IT

WEBSITE

4. _____ . _____ .
   AUTHOR (IF GIVEN)   NAME OF WEB PAGE OR ARTICLE

   _____ . _____
   DATE OF POSTING/REVISION NAME OF ORGANIZATION AFFILIATED WITH SITE

   _____ . _____ .
   ELECTRONIC ADDRESS (URL)   DATE YOU READ IT

BIBLIOGRAPHY/WORKS CITED

Adams, Ernest. *World War II*. Chicago: Harcourt, 2003.

Levy, Patricia. *D-Day*. New York: Marshall Cavendish, 2001.

Paulsen, Mark. *Battle of Normandy*. 2004. *United States and World War II*.
        http://worldwarII.netl. Feb. 3, 2006.

"Punishment of Prisoners of War," *EyeWitness to History, 2001*
        http://www.eyewitnesstohistory.com/. Feb. 24, 2005.

General Rules:

1. Alphabetize entries by author's last name. If there is no author, use the first word of the title (skip A, An, The).
2. Titles are italicized. Double space all lines.
3. Begin each entry at the left margin (1") and indent subsequent lines five spaces from the margin.

Buff

NAME: _____

TEACHER: _____

DATE: _____ PER.: _____

SOURCE PAGE-2 Books, 1 Periodical, 2 Websites

BOOK

1. _____ . _____
   AUTHOR (OR EDITOR)   TITLE of BOOK

   _____ . _____ :
                                     PLACE

   _____ , _____ . PAGES USED: _____ .
   PUBLISHER   YEAR PUBLISHED

   Call Number
   _____
   _____
   _____

BOOK

2. _____ . _____
   AUTHOR (OR EDITOR)   TITLE of BOOK

   _____ . _____ :
                                     PLACE

   _____ , _____ . PAGES USED: _____ .
   PUBLISHER   YEAR PUBLISHED

   Call Number
   _____
   _____
   _____

PERIODICAL

3. _____ . _____ .
   AUTHOR (IF GIVEN)   NAME OF ARTICLE

   _____ . _____ : _____ . _____ .
   NAME OF PERIODICAL (SOURCE)   DATE   PAGES   NAME OF DATABASE

   _____ . _____
   ELECTRONIC ADDRESS (URL)   DATE YOU READ IT

WEBSITE

4. _____ . _____ .
   AUTHOR (IF GIVEN)   NAME OF WEB PAGE OR ARTICLE

   _____ . _____
   DATE OF POSTING/REVISION   NAME OF ORGANIZATION AFFILIATED WITH SITE

   _____ . _____ .
   ELECTRONIC ADDRESS (URL)   DATE YOU READ IT

WEBSITE

5. _____ . _____ .
   AUTHOR (IF GIVEN)   NAME OF WEB PAGE OR ARTICLE

   _____ . _____
   DATE OF POSTING/REVISION   NAME OF ORGANIZATION AFFILIATED WITH SITE

   _____ . _____ .
   ELECTRONIC ADDRESS (URL)   DATE YOU READ IT

BIBLIOGRAPHIC EXAMPLES:

#1–Smith, Ernest. *Alcohol and Teens*. New York: Doubleday, 2003.

#2–*The Encyclopedia of Drugs and Alcohol*. New York: Franklin Watts, 2001.

#3–Frick, Robert. "Investing in Medical Miracles." *Newsweek*. Feb. 1999: 80-87. *SIRS Researcher*. http://www.sirs.com. Feb. 25, 2004.

#4–Jones, Dave. "The Hot Button." Oct. 2006. *Roughcut*. http://www.roughcut.com. Nov. 8, 2006.

Appendix 6

Name:_____ Decade: _____ Category: _____

Topic:_____

Book	Internet
•	•
•	•
•	•
•	•
•	•
_____	_____
Source Number/ Page #	Source Number

Topic:_____

Book	Internet
•	•
•	•
•	•
•	•
•	•
_____	_____
Source Number/ Page #	Source Number

Topic:_____

Book	Internet
•	•
•	•
•	•
•	•
•	•
_____	_____
Source Number/ Page #	Source Number

NAME: _____

TEACHER: _____

DATE: _____ PER.: _____

SOURCE PAGE

ENCYCLOPEDIA

1. _____ . _____
   AUTHOR (IF GIVEN)   TITLE of ARTICLE

_____ . _____
                    TITLE OF ENCYCLOPEDIA

_____ . _____ . PAGES USED: _____ .
                    YEAR PUBLISHED

Call Number
_____
_____
_____

BOOK

2. _____ . _____
   AUTHOR (OR EDITOR)   TITLE of BOOK

_____ . _____ :
                    PLACE

_____ , _____ . PAGES USED: _____ .
PUBLISHER   YEAR PUBLISHED

Call Number
_____
_____
_____

WEBSITE

3. _____ . _____ .
   AUTHOR (IF GIVEN)   NAME OF WEB PAGE OR ARTICLE

_____ . _____
DATE OF POSTING/REVISION   NAME OF ORGANIZATION AFFILIATED WITH SITE

_____ . _____
ELECTRONIC ADDRESS (URL)   DATE YOU READ IT

WEBSITE

4. _____ . _____ .
   AUTHOR (IF GIVEN)   NAME OF WEB PAGE OR ARTICLE

_____ . _____
DATE OF POSTING/REVISION   NAME OF ORGANIZATION AFFILIATED WITH SITE

_____ . _____
ELECTRONIC ADDRESS (URL)   DATE YOU READ IT

BIBLIOGRAPHIC EXAMPLES:

#1–Smith, Ernest. "Leo." *World Book Encyclopedia.* 2007.

#2–Levy, Patricia. *The Zodiac.* San Diego: Lucent, 2006.

#3–"Constellations." 2004. *Peoria Astronomical Society.* http://www.astronomical.org/. Feb. 23, 2007.

#4–"Constellations: Leo" *Hawaiian Astronomical Society.* 2005. http://www.hawastsoc.org/deepsky/leo/index.html. Feb. 23, 2007.

Credits

CHAPTER 1

Stanley, Deborah B. *Practical Steps to the Research Process for High School.* Westport, Conn.: Libraries Unlimited, 1999. 230p. $35. 1–563–08762–6.

CHAPTER 2

Dwight D. Eisenhower Photo: Farm Security Administration—Office of War Information Photograph Collection, Prints and Photographs Division, Library of Congress, LC-USW33–029187-C.

George C. Marshall Photo: Farm Security Administration—Office of War Information Photograph Collection, Prints and Photographs Division, Library of Congress, LC-USW33–038043-C.

"…forever, Amen. Hit the dirt." Cartoon: Copyright 1944 by Bill Mauldin. Courtesy of the Mauldin Estate.

Ernest R. Volkman Photos: By permission, from Volkman family collection.

CHAPTER 3

Star of David Photo: United States Holocaust Museum, courtesy of Fritz Gluckstein.

Adolf Hitler and his aides in Nuremberg, 1934, Photo: In portfolio: Nazi Party Day in Nuremberg, 1934, Prints and Photographs Division, Library of Congress, LC-USZ62–10610.

Jews Captured Photo: United States Holocaust Museum, courtesy of National Archives and Records Administration, College Park.

CHAPTER 4

Negro Sharecropper Photo: Lange, Dorothea, photographer. Farm Security Administration—Office of War Information Photograph Collection, Prints and Photographs Division, Library of Congress, LC-USF34–018181-E.

CHAPTER 5

Celebrating Russian Revolution Photo: Bain Collection, Prints and Photographs Division, Library of Congress, LC-DIG-ggbain-24451.
Karl Marx Photo: Prints and Photographs Division, Library of Congress, LC-USZ62–16530.
Stalin and Lenin Photo: Prints and Photographs Division, Library of Congress, LC-USZ61–2207.

CHAPTER 6

Shakespeare Photo: Prints and Photographs Division, Library of Congress, LC-USZ62–104495.

CHAPTER 10

Edgar Allan Poe Photo: Prints and Photographs Division, Library of Congress, LC-USZ62–10610.
Raven Photo: Theatrical Poster Collection, Prints and Photographs Division, Library of Congress, LC-USZ62–10610.

CHAPTER 11

Cambodian Fisherman Photo: United Nations Photo. Prints and Photographs Division, Library of Congress, LC-USZ62–96896.
Flag of Cambodia Photo: U.S. Department of State Background Note: Cambodia. June 2007. http://www.state.gov/r/pa/ei/bgn/2732.htm.

CHAPTER14

Miners Photo: Prints and Photographs Division, Library of Congress, LC-USZ62–116688.
Prospector Panning Gold Photo: Farm Security Administration—Office of War Information Photograph Collection, Prints and Photographs Division, Library of Congress, LC-USF33–012696-M4.
United States Map Photo: Prints and Photographs Division, Library of Congress, LC-DIG-ppmsca-10758.

CHAPTER 15

Lee Trevino pictures. From personal collection of John Volkman.

CHAPTER 16

Socrates Photo: Bequest of Susan Dwight Bliss, 1966 (67.55.167) New York Metropolitan Museum of Art.

About the Author

JOHN D. VOLKMAN has been the library media teacher at Reedley (California) High School since 2002. He received his MA in library science from San Jose State University in 1976 and has been a library media teacher at Fresno-area high schools since then. His first book was *Cruising through Research; Library Skills for Young Adults* (Libraries Unlimited, 1998). The World War II station unit in the current book has received numerous awards. He is an avid runner (having run close to 100 marathons) and coaches marathon runners for the Leukemia and Lymphoma Society's Team in Training. For close to 20 years he has also been the librarian at The Bridge: Evangelical Free Church, Fresno, which has one of the largest church collections in the country.